Indigenous Materials in Libraries and the Curriculum

Indigenous Materials in Libraries and the Curriculum: Latin American and Latinx Sources argues for a decolonial engagement with Indigenous peoples' creative work to build awareness of divergent epistemologies and foster healing in the learning community.

This book explores how faculty and librarians can collaborate to develop inclusive library collections and curricula by supporting Indigenous peoples' reclamation of lands and languages. The authors present practices to build and disseminate collections that showcase the work of Indigenous creators from Latin America and compensate for historical erasure and misrepresentation. Consideration is also given to developing a non-hegemonic curriculum in Indigenous languages and cultures for faculty and students from multicultural backgrounds, particularly Latinx students of Indigenous descent. Above all, the book aspires to facilitate the participation of Indigenous peoples in the scholarly conversation to counteract epistemic and material extractivism and transform the scaffolding of higher education in the current global climate crisis.

Indigenous Materials in Libraries and the Curriculum is inspired by a transhemispheric vision to elicit conversation between Indigenous peoples from Latin America (Abiayala) and North America (Turtle Island). The book will appeal to academics, librarians, students, and activists interested in Indigenous languages and cultures, decolonization, DEI initiatives, and library collection development policies that prioritize non-hegemonic narratives.

Javier Muñoz-Díaz is a literary and cultural critic. His research focuses on Latin American and Latinx cultural studies, Indigenous and Native American studies, Quechua/Kichwa languages and cultures, Queer/Cuir studies, and environmental humanities. A person of Quechua descent, Muñoz-Díaz is interested in the cultural history and contemporary processes of re-indigenization in the Andes and Amazon regions. Muñoz-Díaz is starting the position of Assistant Professor of Spanish at Farmingdale State College in August 2024.

Kathia Ibacache is assistant professor and Romance languages librarian at the University of Colorado, Boulder. She is interested in advancing collection development with a user-centered approach and focusing on inclusion and diversity. Her research interest encompasses digital accessibility within teaching and learning technologies, collection development, and representing Latin American Indigenous language materials in university libraries.

Leila Gómez is a professor of women and gender studies at the University of Colorado, Boulder. She is the author *of Impossible Domesticity: Travels in Mexico* (Pittsburgh UP, 2021) and several other books. Her recent research focuses on documentaries and films on land issues and environmental justice by Latin American women filmmakers. She started the Quechua Language Program as director of the Latin American and Latinx Studies Center (LALSC) at CU Boulder from 2017 to 2023.

Indigenous Materials in Libraries and the Curriculum

Latin American and Latinx Sources

Javier Muñoz-Díaz,
Kathia Ibacache and
Leila Gómez

LONDON AND NEW YORK

First published 2024
by Routledge
4 Park Square, Milton Park, Abingdon, Oxon OX14 4RN

and by Routledge
605 Third Avenue, New York, NY 10158

Routledge is an imprint of the Taylor & Francis Group, an informa business

© 2024 **Javier Muñoz-Díaz, Kathia Ibacache and Leila Gómez**

The right of **Javier Muñoz-Díaz, Kathia Ibacache and Leila Gómez** to be identified as authors of this work has been asserted in accordance with sections 77 and 78 of the Copyright, Designs and Patents Act 1988.

All rights reserved. No part of this book may be reprinted or reproduced or utilised in any form or by any electronic, mechanical, or other means, now known or hereafter invented, including photocopying and recording, or in any information storage or retrieval system, without permission in writing from the publishers.

Trademark notice: Product or corporate names may be trademarks or registered trademarks, and are used only for identification and explanation without intent to infringe.

British Library Cataloguing-in-Publication Data
A catalogue record for this book is available from the British Library

ISBN: 978-1-032-61849-4 (hbk)
ISBN: 978-1-032-66061-5 (pbk)
ISBN: 978-1-032-66056-1 (ebk)

DOI: 10.4324/9781032660561

Typeset in Times New Roman
by MPS Limited, Dehradun

Contents

Introduction: A Decolonial Engagement with
Indigenous Peoples' Creative Work   1
JAVIER MUÑOZ-DÍAZ AND LEILA GÓMEZ

1 Building an Underrepresented Collection   18
KATHIA IBACACHE

2 Universities Libraries as More Than Repositories
of Information   37
KATHIA IBACACHE

3 How to Decolonize and Indigenize the
Curriculum   48
JAVIER MUÑOZ-DÍAZ AND LEILA GÓMEZ

4 The Power of Healing and Indigenizing Feminism
in the Classroom   62
LEILA GÓMEZ AND JAVIER MUÑOZ-DÍAZ

Epilogue: The Quechua Language Program at the
University of Colorado, Boulder   80
LEILA GÓMEZ

Works Cited   *84*
Index   *91*

Introduction
A Decolonial Engagement with Indigenous Peoples' Creative Work

Javier Muñoz-Díaz and Leila Gómez

Indigenous activists for land and environmental rights are among the most vulnerable communities in the current Anthropocene epoch.[1] Since the rise of neoliberal politics at the end of the 20th century, Latin America has experienced a resurgence of extractive economies that take advantage of the vast natural resources in the region. This political model is called "extractivism," which is "the accelerated extraction of natural resources to satisfy a global demand for mineral and energy and to provide what natural governments consider economic growth" (Blaser and De la Cadena 2). Such a resource-based economic model is prevalent in the whole political spectrum, including right-wing and left-wing governments. Indigenous peoples are systematically harassed, criminalized, and murdered by "necropolitical alliances between the state and corporations" (2).

The number of environmental defenders assassinated in Latin America paints a very disheartening situation. According to a 2022 report by the Cultural Survival organization, about 53 Indigenous activists were murdered that year in Latin America, a region that also comprises three out of four assassinations of environmental defenders worldwide ("In Memoriam"). On the other hand, about 40% of environmental defenders murdered in 2022 were Indigenous, a disproportionately high figure given that Indigenous peoples comprise roughly 6% of the global population ("In Memoriam"). By honoring the humanitarian cost of the Indigenous struggle for sovereignty/authonomy, the authors of this introduction want to challenge diversity, equity, and inclusion (DEI) initiatives in higher education stranded in tokenization or assimilation. We seek to move beyond a metaphorical understanding of decolonization in academia (Tuck and Yang).

It is an urgent but challenging task to incorporate a decolonial approach to university library collections and curricula dealing with Indigenous materials (in the case of this book, with materials related to Latin American and Latinx peoples). The peril of assimilation into power structures hangs over sites of struggle and its demands for transforming

DOI: 10.4324/9781032660561-1

the socioeconomic fabric of higher education. For instance, scholarly work about Indigenous peoples is at risk of harboring knowledge and detaching it from its agents, production systems, and distribution circuits. If library collections and the curriculum are still Eurocentric (grounded on settler/internal colonialism and white supremacy), Indigeneity becomes an ornament without any educational or political impact.

This book, *Indigenous Materials in Libraries and the Curriculum*, wants to participate in current decolonial efforts taking place in higher education by following Silvia Rivera Cusicanqui's motto, "There can be no discourse of decolonization, no theory of decolonization, without a decolonizing practice" (100). We seek to engage with decolonizing practices streaming from Indigenous peoples living in Latin America and Latinx people of Indigenous heritage by promoting collaboration between agents working in academia (librarians and faculty) and agents working in Indigenous materials' system of production and circulation. Thanks to this collaboration grounded in a decolonial framework, current library collection development and curriculum design practices will move beyond materials with a Eurocentric perspective or sanctioned by Global North's distribution systems.[2] Our book strives to showcase underrepresented material related to Indigenous Latin American and Latinx peoples that circulate in alternative, non-hegemonic, and counter-hegemonic distribution systems.

The authors of this introduction want to acknowledge their positionality as scholars working in the U.S. higher education system. We have Latin American origin and maintain personal and professional ties with the Latin American region and its U.S. diaspora (Latinx). However, we recognize that our book is written from a position of material and symbolic privilege conferred by Global North institutions, which are anchored in socioeconomic dynamics of global domination. The pattern of extractivism that stems from European/Eurocentric imperialism is not limited to Global South's natural resources, but it also includes their cultural and symbolic production, ideas, beliefs, and values. As Silvia Rivera Cusicanqui reminds us

> Ideas run, like rivers, from the south to the north and are transformed into tributaries in major waves of thought. But just as in the global market for material goods, ideas leave the country [in the Global South] converted into raw material[s], which become regurgitated and jumbled [by the Global North] in the final product. (104)

Rivera Cusicanqui is referring to rampant inequalities of knowledge production between the Global North and Global South, a disparity that has worsened in the last decades due to market concentration: "The headquarters of the major publishers, the major scholarly journals and the major scientific societies and associations are largely found in the global North" (Collyer 61). Another example of this inequality is the citation count system since "despite the existence of knowledge production in the global South, Southern scholarship is rarely cited by either Northern or Southern scholars" (58).

On a similar note, Indigenous peoples' materials (books, films, digital media, ephemera, among others) are usually reduced to raw materials for the storage and inquiry of Global North university libraries and academic departments. Instead, the authors of this introduction propose that Indigenous peoples are agents of scholarly inquiry who had devised categories of analysis based on, in the words of K'iche' Maya activist/ scholar Emil Keme, "our own cosmogonies and those forms of social cohesion that have been the cornerstone of our survival" (52). *Indigenous Materials in Libraries and the Curriculum* highlights creative works representing Indigenous knowledge as we constantly dialogue with Indigenous scholars, writers, filmmakers, artists, educators, and community leaders. Their work and presence as instructors, speakers, organizers (and not as mere informants or performers) in courses, symposia, and events are paramount to our decolonizing praxis. There is no doubt that we need to create strong alliances between Indigenous and non-Indigenous peoples to transform our institutions radically.

As Emil Keme proposes, such collaborations between Indigenous and non-Indigenous agents should aim to build a civilization project rooted in Indigenous peoples' sovereignty/autonomy and articulated through their locus of political enunciation. Using the category of "Abiayala" ("a transhemispheric Indigenous bridge" based on the Guna people's name for the American continent), Keme outlines

> a dialogue that could potentially develop political alliances in the formation of a new Indigenous and non-Indigenous historical bloc that opposes ideas and civilizational Eurocentric projects like "Latin (America)," "Latinity," or "Americas," as well as extractivist economies based on capitalism and socialism at national, continental, and intercontinental levels. (43)

Indigenous Materials in Libraries and the Curriculum modestly aspires to build bridges and networks that strengthen active and fruitful exchanges. Decolonization is not assimilation or "equal access to participate in capitalist oppression and ideological state apparatuses such as the police and school" (Casey and Jaffee 629), but it is dismantling historical power structures rooted in land dispossession and unequal resource distribution. Such a task "remains unfinished, and is perhaps unfinishable" (Nadarajah and Grydehøj 440), but that does not mean unworthy of pursuing it.

Coloniality of Power and Geopolitics of Knowledge

To advocate for Indigenous knowledge in U.S. academia, we aim to engage with materials *produced by or with Indigenous peoples* rather than materials *about Indigenous peoples*. A decolonial critique confronts the structural distortions in library collections and the curriculum about Indigenous peoples, which exerts epistemic violence grounded in dynamics of land dispossession. For this reason, we are interested in materials produced by Indigenous authors or that showcase Indigenous peoples' agency and perspective. Changing a proposition (*by/with* instead of *about*) seems to be a minor or cosmetic change. However, we embed this proposal in Anibal Quijano's outline of the "coloniality of power." To understand how this global pattern of domination works, we need to review the existing semantic overlapping between "Indigenous" and "Indian" (two terms that sound similar but do not share etymology).[3]

Based on a 1981 study by Special Rapporteur José R. Martínez Cobo, the United Nations defines define "Indigenous peoples" as follows:

> Indigenous communities, peoples and nations are those which, having a historical continuity with pre-invasion and pre-colonial societies that developed on their territories, consider themselves distinct from other sectors of the societies now prevailing on those territories, or parts of them. They form at present non-dominant sectors of society and are determined to preserve, develop and transmit to future generations their ancestral territories, and their ethnic identity, as the basis of their continued existence as peoples, in accordance with their own cultural patterns, social institutions, and legal system.
> ("Permanent Forum on Indigenous Issues")

The United Nation's definition of Indigenous peoples pertains to a legal and administrative framework that must facilitate international affairs. Although such a definition is deliberately vague, it has played a critical role in legislation favorable to Indigenous interests. A landmark example is the International Labor Organization (ILO) Convention 169, which recognizes Indigenous peoples' right to self-determination within a nation-state. For the purpose of this book, we are not focusing on invasion and colonization processes in general terms (ethnic wars have occurred throughout human history) but on those dynamics that stem from the 16th-century European colonization of the Americas. Quijano's "coloniality of power" states that the current global pattern of domination (global capitalism) is based on a racial distinction and geographical distribution that originated in the European invasion of the Americas. Christopher Columbus's voyages (1492–1504) were the starting point of European transatlantic empires (Spain, Portugal, England, France, etc.) that, by the

19th century, reached Africa, Southern Asia, and Oceania, becoming a planetary phenomenon. Europe hosted the metropoles and benefited from extractivism, while the rest of the world experienced colonization processes that, in addition to inflicting exploitation, relegated them to an inferior status (Quijano 542–9). Europeans and settlers of European origin started identifying themselves as Christians, then as white, and finally as modern. In contrast, the native people of the colonized lands were reduced by the colonizing institutions to gentiles, non-white, and pre-modern.

The racialization and subordination of the pair "Indian/Indigenous" as non-European, non-white, and pre-modern arisen from the European invasion and colonization of the Americas. Europeans originally referred to the aboriginal peoples of the Americas as Indios (Indians) since Christopher Columbus thought that his party had arrived in Eastern Asia in 1492. During the Spanish colonization of the Americas, the term "Indian" was a legal concept of the colonial state (Ramírez Zavala 1646) that homogenized all the native populations, blurring the lines of previous ethnic allegiances (Maya, Mexica, Inca, Aymara, etc.) to locate them in a subordinated position (people without pure Christian or Spanish blood). The idiom "blood" does not refer to current ideas of biology and culture, but to an ambiguous and flexible concept related to social hierarchies (estates of the real) and "a moral measure articulated through the classificatory languages of *calidad* [quality], *clase* [class] and *honor*" (De la Cadena 265). By the end of the 18th century, Enlightenment ideas changed the European perception of Indians: "The turn to natural science and the practices of visual recording gave the notion of embodied difference a new tangibility […]. Through the empiricist objectification of the world, Enlightenment science forged the first images of Indians as visible, measurable bodies" (Majluf 22). In other words, the present-day binary race/culture appears, attaching the former to biology/physic and the later to ethnicity/spirit. The term "Indian" left a religious and legal framework to enter the scientific discourse.

The overlapping of Indian and Indigenous happened in the wake of Enlightenment. The term *Indigenous* first appeared in Spanish dictionaries in 1492 with the meaning of "natural de allí" (native from there) and was predominately used for the natural world, namely plants that belong to or originally sprout in a specific land. No explicit connection existed between the words Indigenous and Indian until, by the end of the 18th century, a French dictionary defined "Indigène" as the native population of the Americas (Ramírez Zavala 1644–5). A few decades later, German naturalist Alexander von Humboldt used Indigenous as synonym of Indian in his highly influential 1811 *Political essay on the kingdom of New Spain* (Ramírez Zavala 1659).

The recently independent Latin American countries would use "Indigenous" instead of "Indian" since the legal framework of the ancient regime had disappeared. Significantly, the category Indigenous participated in a new homogenization process in a postcolonial context. Liberal criollo elites (the descendants of Spaniards that led the 19th-century independence process) employed the term "Indigenous" to standardize the native population (Ramírez Zavala 1663) and subjugated them to a Eurocentric modernization/acculturation process.

We want to highlight that the pair "Indian/Indigenous," besides referring to the original people from the continent nowadays called the Americas, has functioned as an inverted mirror image of the people who crossed the Atlantic Sea and carried out the colonization process. For their part, these people, the colonizers, started identifying themselves as "Europeans." In addition to the stark differences between "Indian/Indigenous" and "European" peoples (who belong to different geographies), they were also located in a hierarchic relationship. An artistic piece that clearly shows the formation of both geo-political identities is Johannes Stradanus's *Allegory of America* (c. 1587–9), a drawing that illustrates the European invasion of the Americas by means of a wealthy and fully dressed man (Amerigo Vespucci) waking up a naked and submissive woman.[4] The odd couple divides the picture into two sections, each of them showcasing entities and objects associated with each character. The man stands straight with a flag and cross atop of a staff. The man also carries a compass while imposing ships approach the shore in the background. Next to him, the woman is surrounded by a lavish nature and mischievous animals. In the distance, a group of naked people are eating human flesh at a campfire (Figure 0.1).

Figure 0.1 *Allegory of America* (c. 1587–89), Johannes Stradanus.

This drawing's expressive narrative is not limited to the distinct attributes of each figure, but it sprouts from the power relationship established between them. Both figures illustrates a binary between culture and nature, mind and body, knowledge and ignorance, civilization and savagery, European and non-European, male and female. Following the "coloniality of gender" (Lugones), we identify that the gender divide in the *Allegory of America* is consubstantial to the racial divide that stems from the European invasion of the Americas. The European ideal subject is a white man, while the non-European subjects are racialized and feminized as inferior.

Certainly, it is difficult to overestimate the impact of Columbus's enterprise on the material and symbolic scaffolding of our world system. However, a lesser-discussed issue is that we know a great deal about Columbus's enterprise and very little about the Taino people living in the present-day Caribbean region. Here we are not simply pointing out that the vision of the European conqueror prevailed over the vision of the Indigenous vanquished. The problem with such a perspective is that it implies ideologies of cultural superiority. Instead, we want to address the issue that Columbus's written accounts and other materials produced by his party were stored, quoted, paraphrased, and disseminated by European institutions of knowledge production. On the other hand, these institutions systematically dismissed Indigenous accounts, even if they employed Eurocentric writing technologies and techniques. The authors of this introduction believe that a decolonial approach to how knowledge is stored and distributed is indispensable to counteract such discursive/symbolic disparages, which are grounded in a history of material dispossession. As Ramos and Daly point out, "decoloniality does not have to do with the question alone of *what* we see, but performs a questioning of *why* we see things the way we do" (xxv–xxvi). Returning to Stradanus's *Allegory of America*, we need to locate the drawing into a system of accumulation and distribution that privileged Eurocentric perspectives about Indigenous peoples as objects of intellectual inquiry rather than agents of knowledge production.

An example of Indigenous people as agents of knowledge is Felipe Guamán Poma de Ayala's "Regidores: Tenga Libro Qvipo, Cv(en)ta," one of the several drawings that composed the *The First New Chronicle and Good Government* (c. 1615). The drawing presents a character (the regidor, a council member) dressed in male Indigenous attire and standing tall in a dignified position. The character is looking carefully at an open book held in his left hand while his right hand manipulates a set of strings extending from his belt to the floor. This last object is a quipu, an ancient Andean recording device that uses cords and knots to store and disseminate knowledge. The regidor employs two highly different but complementary technologies (one native quipu and the

Figure 0.2 "Regidores: Tenga Libro Qvipo, Cv(en)ta," The First New Chronicle and Good Government (c. 1605), Felipe Guamán Poma de Ayala.

imported book) to fulfill his duties in the colonial system established after the Spanish invasion of the Andes (Figure 0.2).

Indigenous chronicler Guamán Poma de Ayala wrote *The First New Chronicle and Good Government* as a letter to Philip II, King of Spain, to denounce the destruction of Indigenous people's livelihood in the wake of the Spanish colonization of current-day Peru. Due to the misrule and rampage abuses, Indigenous people were living in an upside-down world. Interestingly, this book-length letter is also a defense of Indigenous political institutions, which ruled the land sagaciously before the arrival of the Spaniards. Poma de Ayala was a devout Christian who recognized the authority of the Spanish monarchy, but he also showcased Indigenous claims to recover their political sovereignty. What is important to highlight here is that such a radical political claim relies on the defense of Indigenous systems of production, storage, and distribution of knowledge. Since the Andean quipu stands on equal footing with the European book, Indigenous knowledge production recovers a legitimacy stripped away by the coloniality of power.

Inspired by Guaman Poma's analogy between the *quipu* and the book, the authors of this introduction want to endorse Emil Keme's proposal of "Abiayala" as a locus of Indigenous political enunciation "to interpellate a collectivity of Indigenous nations, as well as non-Indigenous allies that struggle to transcend the conditions of internal/external colonialisms and their logics of elimination" (46). While the civilizational projects epitomized by the ideas of "America" and "Latin America" imply the extermination/assimilation of Indigenous peoples, "Abiayala" is concerned with articulating a collective Indigenous subjectivity based on common experiences of marginalization. In Keme's words, "By positioning ourselves as Indigenous subjects, we can not only enable the hegemonic articulation of our demands but also negotiate with non-Indigenous others to secure the constitution of multicultural or intercultural national and international models based on our own Indigenous needs and perspectives" (58). The aim of incorporating material by/with Indigenous peoples into libraries and the curriculum must be to serve better counter-hegemonic civilizational projects such as "Abiayala."

We are fully aware of the convoluted history of Indigenous materials related to resistance movements and political claims. Guamán Poma de Ayala's book-length letter to the Spanish king is currently stored in the Royal Danish Library (Denmark), while most of the surviving quipus are located in the Ethnological Museum of Berlin (Germany). Since these Indigenous materials are stored in Global North institutions, the research produced by these institutions or under their sponsorship obtains epistemological privilege—it is considered cutting-edge and is widely cited. This is the geopolitics of knowledge in action. We believe that Indigenous materials should return to their original lands and participate in the circuits of knowledge production and distribution that are specific to them. In the meantime, efforts must be made to prevent similar material and epistemological plundering. Although *Indigenous Materials in Libraries and in the Curriculum* promotes the acquisition of Indigenous literature and film materials as valuable agents of knowledge in academic institutions, we also advocate for returning Indigenous historical works to their Indigenous lands. Global North's institutions might claim that they have the best preservation conditions and offer several opportunities to access the materials—for instance, the Royal Danish Library digitized *The First New Chronicle and Good Government*, making it accessible worldwide. However, one can use the same argument to support the return of Indigenous materials to their original land—scholars could still access those materials using the technology available to us. Without the reclamation of Indigenous materials and their insertion in Indigenous epistemologies, the current modern/colonial geopolitics of knowledge will continue.

Language Reclamation and Pluriversal Knowledge

Our aim to foster decolonization in higher education is aligned with efforts for "language reclamation" throughout Abiayala. As Myaamia linguist Wesley Y. Leonard argues, the distinction between "language revitalization" and "language reclamation" stems from engaging with Indigenous epistemologies (their understanding of what language means and does) and contemporary needs determined by community agents (19). While "revitalization" usually describes a top-down model based on Eurocentric epistemologies (articulated by the academic fields of linguistics and anthropology), "reclamation" is a form of decolonial praxis "which entails identifying and resisting the imposition of Western values and knowledge systems that contribute to the subjugation of Indigenous peoples" (16).

Language reclamation is not limited to increasing the number of speakers of a minoritized language; instead, it is concerned with the placement of creative language use within a broader frame of cultural practices and political claims. In that sense, language reclamation implies an understanding of Indigenous languages as historical and political constructs that involve a wide array of practitioners in different contexts (rural, urban, digital, etc.). This multilayered approach moves away from essentializing perspectives about Indigenous languages as "fixed" and "immutable," such as the linguistic ideology of "ruralization"—a believe that "authentic" Indigenous language speakers are monolingual and live in isolated rural environments (Andrade Ciudad et al. 153). Instead, Indigenous languages and cultures break through colonizing dynamics and establish their global presence and potentialities.[5]

We want to use the principles of "language reclamation" to outline our approach to decolonizing Indigenous materials in library collections and curricula. Our aim is not limited to increasing the number of Indigenous materials stored in libraries or included in course assignments. This book also seeks to engage with the systems of production, distribution, and reception in which those materials appear, including the cultural and epistemological values attached to them. In order to recognize Indigenous voices and epistemology in the production and dissemination of their materials, we need to foster a decolonization of academic institutions.

In *Decolonizing the University*, Cameroonian philosopher Achilles Mbembe follows Kenyan writer Ngugi wa Thiong'o and the Latin American thinker Enrique Dussell to make three important points in a decolonization project. The first one is to put native languages at the center of the university's teaching and learning projects. Since Mbembe refers to Africa, these languages are Swahili, isiZulu, isiXhosa, Shona, Yoruba, Hausa, Lingala, and Gikuyu. In a North American university, these languages are Navajo, Cherokee, Cree, Arapaho, Lakota, and

Nahuatl, among more than hundreds. We believe that the decolonization of Latin American studies centers and programs in the U.S. academia should expand teaching languages beyond Spanish and Portuguese to Mayan, Quechua, Guarani, Mapudungun, Aymara, Zapotec, etc. This is not to omit the teaching of non-native languages beyond English—a decolonized university will teach French, Portuguese, Arabic, Mandarin, Hindi, etc. For Mbembe, "Colonialism rhymes with monolingualism. The African university of tomorrow will be multilingual" (35).

The second point Mbembe states is that decolonizing the university requires a geographical imagination that extends well beyond the confines of the nation-state, or following Thiong'o's work, "well beyond the geographical limits of the continent" (36). Something along the lines can be said for Latin American Indigenous geographies, whose speakers migrate worldwide, particularly to the United States, where Indigenous languages are spoken in communities outside their original territories. Latin American internationalism, African internationalism, and their intersections with "various other forms of internationalism could help in rethinking the spatial politics of decolonization in so far as true decolonization, as Dubois intimated in 1919, necessarily centers on 'the destiny of humankind' and not of one race, color or ethnos" (Mbembe 36).

For a third point, Mbembe draws from Latin American thinkers' critique of "epistemic coloniality," that is

> the endless production of theories that are based on European traditions. These are produced nearly always by Europeans or Euro-American men who are the only ones accepted as capable of reaching universality; they involve a particular process of knowing about Others ... that never fully acknowledges these Others as thinking and knowledge producing subjects. (37)

The present academic model is based on the universalism of European/European-American science and knowledge. In order to decolonize the university, it is necessary that universal thought becomes pluriversal, and Indigenous languages play a major role in the process.

Teaching Indigenous languages means teaching Indigenous epistemes that contribute to pluriversal knowledge. Mario Blaser and Marisol de la Cadena define "pluriverse" as "heterogeneous worldlings coming together as a political ecology of practices, negotiating their difficulty of being together in heterogeneity" (4). This perspective questions hegemonic ideologies of multiculturalism based on "one-world" that recognizes other worlds' cultural differences and assimilates them. Since such a "one-world" has granted itself the attributes of universality and neutrality, it decides what counts as "knowledge," "culture," and "politics." For instance, when Quechua people claim that a Peruvian Andean mountain is a political stakeholder in land and environmental struggle, "one world" regards such an Indigenous perspective as an example of "cultural difference" rather than an actual political claim (Blase and De la Cadena 2). In multiculturalism, Indigenous epistemologies are recognized as "different," but they are also domesticated and stripped of transformative energy.

In contrast, "pluriverse" engages with the incommensurability and excess that characterize cross-cultural exchange. Rather than recognizing differences, the "pluriverse" participates in the divergence of practices and knowledges that lacks an authoritative center of disciplinary control. According to Blesser and De la Cadena, "excesses across knowledges (ours and others') and hence not-knowing (as we and they usually know) may be an important condition of dialogues that allow for a form of understanding that does not require sameness, and therefore rather than canceling divergence is constituted by it" (10). For instance, Indigenous languages hold key concepts stemming from traditional lifestyles and worldviews, including "botanical, biological, and geographic information and insight into human cognition" (Fernando et al. 49). As journalist Russ Rymer points out, some knowledge that is language-specific and that does not translate successfully to other languages includes medicinal plants, food cultivation, irrigation techniques, navigation systems, and seasonal calendars (qtn. in Gantt 15). By highlighting pluriversal knowledge, we engage with Indigenous epistemologies and materials without reducing their specificities and misrepresenting their claims.

Llorenç Comajoan-Colomé and Serafín M. Coronel-Molina argue that language revitalization (which we prefer to call "reclamation") should have an integral and multilayered scope—it is related to bilingual, multilingual, and multicultural education, as well as second and heritage language teaching and learning (897–904). This overarching perspective clearly contrasts with the history of Indigenous language teaching in U.S. academia, which had a utilitarian perspective that regarded Indigenous languages as resources. In the case of Quechua, Américo Mendoza-Mori explains that.

> Quechua was mostly taught to anthropology or archaeology students who needed to do fieldwork in South America. Additionally, the hiring of Quechua instructors was ad hoc and typically was at the request of a standing faculty member, rather than as part of a comprehensive language program. Also, Quechua instructors then had little room for innovation and almost no job security; they typically were viewed as faculty members' assistants and could be easily removed at any time.

Introduction 13

In this book, *Indigenous Materials in Libraries and the Curriculum*, we state that our role as researchers, librarians, and instructors is to design and implement collaborative strategies with Indigenous peoples, where they are treated as equals and not as informants. Language loss is an index of the genocide perpetuated and still prolonged against Indigenous peoples. As Chickasaw citizen Kari A. B. Chew explains, language reclamation/revitalization is a step toward healing the historical trauma, ensuring survival, and affirming the pluriversality of knowledge (qtn. in Gantt 15).

Overview of Chapters

Collaboration and interdisciplinarity are at the core of this book, where a team of one academic librarian and two faculty members came together to relate experiences and approaches to collection development and curriculum building. While the first two chapters are concerned with library collections and the last two with curriculum and teaching, they all imply and promote the amalgamation of librarian and faculty expertise. Each chapter's outline is based on the circulation system that materials follow in university library collections: from stakeholders in publishing and film production to liaison librarians (Chapter 1), from liaison librarians to faculty and students (Chapter 2), and from faculty to students in curriculum design (Chapter 3) and teaching methodologies (Chapter 4).

The first chapter, "Building an Underrepresented Collection," outlines some principles to promote a library collection that engages with underrepresented materials by Indigenous peoples. The chapter claims the importance of moving beyond storing books or films about Indigenous people; instead, library collections should engage with the array of materials produced by Indigenous authors. The former practice reproduces colonizing dynamics, while the latter would allow students and the general population to acknowledge and participate in Indigenous epistemologies. These epistemologies have endured the hardships of colonization and articulate counter-hegemonic practices, such as Potawatomi's vision of nature as a "gift" rather than raw material and commodity. Drawing from Ibacache's experience as a liaison librarian, the chapter outlines four principles: 1) the nuances in Indigenous identities, 2) literary genres, 3) target group, and 4) timeline flexibility. Moreover, librarians should engage with stakeholders in the book and film businesses apart from hegemonic or mainstream publishers. The chapter promotes interprofessional collaborations that engage directly with Indigenous authors or participate in alternative systems of distribution (libreros, book fairs, etc.).

While the first chapter discusses how university libraries should reach out to the distribution system of Indigenous materials, the second chapter deals with enhancing Indigenous materials' visibility and accessibility to students and the general population. "Universities Libraries as More than Repositories of Information" outlines the liaison librarian role as a "cultural broker" whose duties are not limited to serving research faculty needs. Instead, the liaison librarian should play two important roles in students' academic and professional growth: 1) to facilitate the interaction with underrepresented Indigenous materials and 2) to promote the development of students' cross-cultural skills. By repurposing the liaison librarian practice called "window framework for the acquisition," this chapter proposes an "open window" as a metaphor for the cross-cultural opportunities that arise from students' engagement with underrepresented materials. The chapter then moves to the issue of the discoverability of Indigenous materials, which is usually hindered by search engines' limitations for multilingual works. Finally, the chapter makes a case for the importance of building a print collection in addition to a digital one. Digital collections have increased over the years (especially after the COVID-19 pandemic), and Indigenous books have a limited print run. However, having both a digital and a print collection benefits Indigenous publishing and production companies and enhances students' cross-cultural awareness and skills.

After covering library collection issues in the first two chapters, Chapters 3 and 4 delve into the faculty's role in disseminating Indigenous materials and facilitating students' engagement with them in and outside of the classroom. Chapter 3, "How to Decolonize and Indigenize the Curriculum," builds upon the concept of "coloniality of the curriculum" (Fúnez-Flores) to underline how the formation of a literary canon is not only concerned with cultural values but with social relations in a geopolitical order that privilege Eurocentric institutions. "Decolonization of the curriculum" is less involved with including some Indigenous authors to the canon but with transforming the scaffolding of knowledge storage and distribution. The chapter then moves to criticize Hispanismo ideology in U.S. Spanish language programs. This ideology prevents the inclusion of materials non-written in Spanish in the curricula, causing the alienation of Latinx materials written in English and Indigenous materials written in Indigenous languages. Drawing from Muñoz-Díaz's experience teaching Latin American and Latinx film courses in the United States, this chapter discusses the challenges and opportunities of conducting such a course in Spanish or English. On the other hand, Latin American and Latinx studies programs seem to be a more suitable venue for those materials; however, mestizaje and indigenous ideologies pervade this interdisciplinary field by prioritizing nation-state belongings. Finally, the chapter discusses how to incorporate Indigenous materials beyond the disciplinary boundaries of linguistics and anthropology.

Indigenous epistemologies about human and other-than-human entities would not only enrich STEM fields but could also challenge Eurocentric understandings of "science" and "technology."

Chapter 4, "The Power of Healing and Indigenizing Feminism in the Classroom," revolves around the instructor's role in facilitating students' engagement with Indigenous materials in and outside the classroom. The chapter proposes "healing" as the ultimate goal of intercultural exchange between students of all backgrounds and Indigenous materials in Indigenous languages. In contrast to assimilationist perspectives, "healing" implies the recognition of colonizing dynamics that are rooted in land dispossession and cultural erasure. Furthermore, following a Critical Latinx Indigeneities paradigm, the chapter connects Indigenous land dispossession in Abiayala to contemporary forced migration to the United States as a continual consequence of settler colonialism and imperialism (Saldaña-Portillo 143). On the other hand, "healing" recognizes the incommensurability of cultural exchanges and points out that Global North theories are unfit to understand Indigenous epistemologies and practices. Drawing from Gómez's experience teaching gender and indigeneity from a transnational perspective, the chapter provides examples of Latin American and Latinx films that address Indigenous women's and sexual dissidence struggles in Abiayala, establishing points of encounter with U.S. Native American documentaries and texts. Films such as *Daughter of the Lake* and *Mothers of the Land* show the linkage between women's rights and environmental rights. On the other hand, Muñoz-Díaz's courses use the film *Retablo* to showcase the entwinement between linguistic colonization and repression of sexual diversity.

The book ends with an epilogue promoting Indigenous initiatives in higher education by sharing the experience of the Quechua Language Program at the University of Colorado at Boulder. To foster a decolonization of the curriculum, this program set up three tasks: 1) hiring a full-time instructor; 2) developing specialized teaching materials; and 3) enhancing interdisciplinary course offering, study abroad opportunities, and event planning. The Quechua Language Program aims to support better underrepresented students and Colorado's growing Latinx Indigenous population.

Materials related to Indigenous peoples are incredibly complex but urgently needed in our current Anthropocene epoch. Our book aims to offer a comprehensive look at issues related to Latin American and Latinx Indigenous materials in libraries and the curriculum, but we also admit several limitations related to the authors' positionality and expertise. Notwithstanding the pervasive impact of coloniality/modernity, Indigenous peoples from Latin America are not a monolithic group with a clear-cut set of characteristics, but they are a plethora of communities with a wide array of cultural traits in permanent interaction with the rest of the world. However, most cases collected in this book are about Indigenous peoples from South America, particularly the Andes and Southern Cone regions. On a similar note, the examples about Indigeneity in the diaspora (Latinx communities) mostly revolve around people of Quechua descent. Our book lacks examples of Indigenous peoples in Mesoamerica or the Amazon rainforest (among other regions) as well as a discussion of the intersections between Indigeneity, Blackness, and other global diasporas. Although our book acknowledges the strong connection between land dispossession and migration, we do not center our analysis on U.S. Latinx Indigenous migration exclusively. Despite these scope limitations, we are confident that *Indigenous Materials in Libraries and the Curriculum* will open similar initiatives about Indigenous peoples from other areas of Latin America, the Americas, and worldwide, and will strengthen the bridges of communication among Latin American Indigenous, Latinx Indigenous, and Native American studies.

Finally, this book favors the denominator Indigenous as an umbrella term over other denominators such as Native, First Nation, or Aboriginal. Since Indigenous is primarily used in Latin America and its global diaspora (Latinx), we decided to sustain it throughout the book. However, we will use the appropriate legal denominator when speaking about a specific ethnicity/nationality from a territory outside or within Abiayala.

Notes

1 "Anthropocene" describes the ongoing geological period in Earth, which is recognizable by newer stratigraphic markers located in glacier ice or lake sediments. These markers are evidence of the impact of humankind in global patterns of environment and climate. As for the starting point to the Anthropocene, the data collected leads to either the 17th or 20th century (Lewis y Maslin). Since those dates coincide with the development of the global system of coloniality/modernity, some scholars prefer to describe this epoch as "Capitaloscene" (Moore). See also Tallbear, "A Sharpening of the Already Present: Settler Apocalypse 2020."

2 In this book, we are using the term Global North to identify what was traditionally understood as the Western World. Since European nations that carried out the colonization of the globe (16th to 20th centuries) are located in the Northern Hemisphere, they became the Global North. These same nations also sustained modernization processes that were imposed as the global standard for development (from 18th century to present day). On the other hand, most of the colonized and underdeveloped/developing nations are located by the Southern Hemisphere (Latin America, Africa, Middle East, Asia, Oceania) and become the Global South. However, this geographical divide between north and south only refers to a general tendency (colonizer/colonized, develop/developing) and is not an absolute marker. Native American peoples and First Nations of Canada are part of the Global South

although their ancestral lands are in the Northern Hemisphere. Similarly, since Australia is a settler-colonial nation like the United States or Canada, it belongs to the Global North although it is located in the Southern Hemisphere.
3 Natalia Majluf points out, following Raúl Alcides Reissner, that "although these terms [Indigenous and Indian] are generally synonymous in Latin America, they are not etymologically related" (180).
4 Natalia Majluf asserts that "The schematic prints and figures that illustrate early chronicles and travel accounts do not quite refer to the concept of the Indian, but rather to the category of the noble or ignoble savage, a complex figure of the early modern European imagination. While they were meant to evoke the New World's indigenous populations, the conventional, allegorical plumed figures that appear on maps and in paintings and books actually personify America as one among other equally abstract representations of the continents. They designate geographic concepts or charged notions of savagery and paganism that do not directly suggest the ideas of cultural difference that are key to modern definitions of the Indian" (20). Although it is pivotal to historicize and differentiate pre-Enlightenment and post-Enlightenment representations of native peoples, we are interested in highlighting the rise and continuity of power dynamics between European and non-European subject positions, which are outlined in *Allegory of America* and continue nowadays.
5 An example of bottom-up language policy and practice efforts are Quechua-language reclamation initiatives in the diaspora. These reclamation initiatives "serve local immigrant communities while also joining hemispheric conversations to advance the language" (Mendoza-Mori and Sprouse 141). In other words, "the future of Quechua is not only in the Andes, but also in the urban spaces of New York, Miami, Salt Lake City, and Philadelphia" (Mendoza-Mori 54).

1 Building an Underrepresented Collection

Kathia Ibacache

In 2019, as a newly appointed Romance languages librarian at the University of Colorado Boulder, I was revising orders received through the Suggest a Library Purchase form sent by a doctoral student from the Department of Spanish and Portuguese.[1] This student was using the form avidly, indicating either a well-involved student or a collection gap that I needed to address—upon inviting the student to my office, they candidly informed me that the collections lacked literary representation of works written by Indigenous authors.

This revelation unlocked the conception of one impactful collection development initiative at a predominantly white university campus in the United States to grow a collection of Indigenous literature from Latin America.[2] This initiative underscores one path for supporting cross-cultural exchange, decolonization, and healing through a library collection that builds bridges among authors of Indigenous literature, book vendors, librarians, and ultimately the readers. My conversation with this student initiated a friendship that eventually led to a collaboration on this book and my commitment to intentionally supporting the revitalization of Indigenous languages and cultures from Latin America through collection development.

This chapter discusses the pathways to build an Indigenous literature and film collection utilizing selection criteria that ensure these collections' Indigenous agency and perspective. These materials represent works written, directed, or produced by Indigenous authors and film creators and those involved with Indigeneity from the viewpoint of Indigenous peoples. By highlighting the Indigenous nature of a collection, we distinguish it from materials about Indigenous people written from an archeological and ethnographic approach where the Indigenous person is the subject of study instead of the content creator. Understanding this contrast is essential to appreciate that the Indigenous creative, literary, and cinematic output carries a distinctive voice and plots near Indigenous communities' experiences. Access to this lens is critical for students to value cultures other than their own.

We will also examine the publisher and book vendor system that brings Indigenous literature into the university library collection. This chapter highlights the roles of small publishers, libraries, and *libreros* (book vendors). A glimpse into these roles will help readers understand the path librarians follow to acquire books considered Indigenous. Then, we note that interprofessional relationships and collaboration among publishers, authors, libreros, and librarians are symbiotically beneficial and impactful. This chapter concludes that building and disseminating collections that showcase Indigenous literature and film has beneficial repercussions for creating curriculum and facilitates students' access to materials not represented in hegemonic curricular settings.

Building a Literature Collection That Is Indigenous

In a conversation with Cherokee author and teacher Daniel Heath Justice, he is asked, Why does Indigenous literature matter? Justice answered:

> Literature is our voiced expression of being in the world, and it enters a world where we are presumed to already be erased or where we are expected to disappear. Our stories, our fiction, our plays, our poems, our songs, all of these embodied story-ways affirm the rightness of our belonging in a world that is so wounded, and so ruptured, but to which we still hold a significant claim. (Hanson 117–18)

A collection of Indigenous literature wants to capture the voice that Justice addresses in his description. This literature comprises authors communicating Indigenous traditional knowledge, the voice of ancestors, and an identity that is in peril trying to survive the loss of land, language, and culture. In *Braiding Sweetgrass: Indigenous Wisdom, Scientific Knowledge, and the Teaching of Plants*, Potawatomi botanist Robin Wall Kimmerer notes that regardless of significant loss, Native peoples' identity to the land is not surrendered. Kimmerer writes, "Our lands were where our responsibility to the world was enacted, sacred grounds. It belonged to itself; it was a gift, not a commodity, so it could never be bought or sold" (17). Latin American Indigenous literature bestows on us as a gift this connection to Earth, its "non-human kinfolk," and the voice of being in the world.[3]

A gift, which the Merriam-Webster online thesaurus identifies, among other terms, is a donation, an offering, and a contribution. A gift is thus defined as something given without the expectation of payment. However, some might argue that a book a library purchases for their constituents is not a gift. Kimmerer refers to a gift economy based on reciprocity as something that must "circulate back" and compares it to a market economy based on commodity and money value (25–30). For example, if a tree gives us fruit, one waters it, nurtures it, and cares for it in a relationship based on gratitude and reciprocity.[4] The gift-giving practice that Kimmerer considers underscores the act of giving, receiving, and reciprocating.[5] In the example of the tree, it provides us food, habitat for other plants and animals, protection from heat, air quality, and tranquility when we are near them. We receive these gifts, and in mutual dependence, we nurture the tree in a symbiotically beneficial cycle.

This mutually beneficial cycle is what readers find when they engage with different ways of knowing by reading an Indigenous book they purchased or a book a library purchased for free access to constituents. Readers receive a gift by immersing in non-hegemonic narratives that open minds to a different type of knowledge, traditional knowledge. Through Indigenous wisdom, which has developed over millennia, we learn about the natural world and the knowledge that comes from it. Indigenous literature, including what we traditionally call fiction and non-fiction works, is one way to access this knowledge and learn, for example, about land conservation and sustainability approaches, holistic ecological management, and spiritual connections to the environment and all living beings. One could reciprocate by broadening our understanding of other cultures than our own and being mindful of Indigenous knowledge as we are part of a multi-cultural, multi-language, and multi-knowledge world.

With this background in mind, we must determine what Indigenous literature is. The notion of Indigenous literature is unclear to many people, as defining this collection poses challenges. Nonetheless, the unmistakable grammatical distinction between the prepositions *about* and *by* (Indigenous people) helps us pave the way for characterizing what an Indigenous literature collection from Latin America should signify. Establishing this clarification is the first step librarians should take to rationalize what type of books they would like to consider for building a collection of Indigenous literature. This contextual step will help librarians with collection development decision-making during the assessment, selection, and acquisition process.

We propose that an Indigenous literature collection from Latin America has the creative output of Indigenous authors and authors writing in an Indigenous language or a European language (primarily Spanish, Portuguese, and English), relating to Indigeneity from the Indigenous people's viewpoint or presenting topics that matter to them. This definition considers more authors than those who self-identify as Indigenous because there are writers in Latin America who, without being Indigenous, write in Indigenous languages or have a *mestizo* identity (a mixed heritage that combines Spanish and Indigenous heritages) and express topics deeply connected with Indigenous communities. The definition we proposed is not exclusive; Indigenous literature from Latin America will likely continue progressing along with societal changes.

Inclusive Selection Criteria

The first selection criterium when building an Indigenous literature collection is the nuances connected to authors. For example, the term mestizo applies to two canonical Peruvian authors (José María Arguedas and César Vallejo) regarded as champions of the Quechua people since their literary work conveys Indigenous epistemologies and denounces their historical oppression. However, due to geopolitical and biographical circumstances, these writers had different ethnicities and linguistic backgrounds. José María Arguedas (1911–1969) was not an Indigenous person but a misti (white mestizo) who learned Quechua and Spanish simultaneously. Arguedas grew up in the rural Peruvian southern Andes, the region with the most significant population of monolingual Quechua speakers at the time. Although Arguedas wrote most of his indigenista novels in Spanish, he also translated Quechua oral literature to Spanish and published original poetic works in Quechua and Spanish. In a famous discourse as an epilogue of his posthumous novel, *The Fox from Up-Above* and *The Fox from Down-Below*, Arguedas identified himself as "I am not an acculturated man; I am a Peruvian who, like a cheerful demon, proudly speaks in Christian and in Indian, in Spanish and Quechua" (269).

On the other hand, the Peruvian poet César Vallejo (1892–1938) was not a white misti but a mestizo writer who can be racialized as Indigenous.[6] Vallejo grew up only learning Spanish since the region where he was born (the rural Peruvian northern Andes) had a minor Indigenous language-speaking population. Although Vallejo only wrote Spanish literature and lived most of his adult life in a European exile, his work is regarded as a milestone in showcasing Indigenous epistemologies (combined with Roman Catholic themes and Marxist ideology) and defending Indigenous people's well-being. José María Arguedas noted, "Vallejo was the beginning and the end" (259). Arguedas and Vallejo exemplify authors whose life experiences helped them intimately understand the plight of the Quechua people from Peru and express it through their writing without culturally appropriating elements from the Quechua culture.

Other authors represent Indigenous monolingual writers who do not write in an Indigenous language, such as the Mapuche poet David Aniñir, whose parents migrated from their ancestral lands to Santiago, Chile's capital (Echeverría, "Three Mapunky Poems"). Aniñir's poetry book, *Mapurbe*, first, interlaces elements of protest for those living in poverty and suffering discrimination in the mouth of the Mapocho River in Santiago, and second, highlights the interculturality between the campesino identity and the urban Mapuche (Aniñir 14–15). These topics are of interest for curricular and research exploration and, thus, due representation in academic libraries.[7]

However, Aniñir's creative output not only represents Indigenous migrant experiences. This poet is remarkable as he transmits in raw and visceral prose the straining realities of Indigenous identity colliding with that of the mestizo country.[8] Aniñir's lines in his poem "Kiñe" refer to the poet himself dressed in jeans and T-shirts with logos from American universities, creating a confused mixture between the "norteameraucano" and the "mapurbe" (Aniñir 28). The neologism "Norteameraucano" combines the terms "Araucano" (Mapuche people from the Araucanía region in Chile) and "norteamericano" people from the United States (Aniñir 28; Echeverría 12).[9] Aniñir uses the word "mezcla" (mix) to denote interculturality, a circumstance connected to most Indigenous peoples and a 21st-century world characterized by the exodus of people. Thus, Aniñir exemplifies Indigenous authors who publish in the dominant language and whose intercultural identity connects with diasporic Indigenous people who moved from their ancestral lands to urban cities.

Another author nuance for selection criterium is self-identified Indigenous authors who write in their ancestral tongue, such as the Zapotec poet Irma Piñeda Santiago, the Mapuche poet Graciela Huinao, the interdisciplinary artist and Quechua and Aymara speaker Elvira Espejo Ayca, and Mayan writer Enriqueta Lunez to name a few. Many of these authors are bilingual and publish their works in bilingual and trilingual editions that some scholars identify as a cultural bridge among cultures.[10] This acknowledgment takes us to another point. An Indigenous literature collection from Latin America will also broadly represent bilingual and trilingual works.

Fortunately, there is a boom in literary works published in multilanguage editions, especially in the 21st century. Books such as *Bínÿbe Oboyejuayëng/Danzantes del Viento* by Hugo Jamioy Juagibioy in Camsá and Spanish; *Poetry of the Earth: Trilingual Mapuche Anthology*, edited by Jaime Huenún Villa in Quechua, English, and Spanish; *Iníi ichí* a book of poetry by Celerina Patricia in Mixtec and Spanish; *Walinto*, poetry by Graciela Huinao, a trilingual edition in Mapudungun, Spanish, and English; *Nahualliandoing dos*, an anthology of poetry in Nahuatl, Spanish, and English; and *Sk'Eoj Jme'Tiku/Cantos de Luna*, a bilingual poetry book in Tsotsil and Spanish by Enriqueta Lunez, are a sample of the prosperous Indigenous literature in multilingual editions.

Significantly, not all self-identified Indigenous authors write for a mainstream audience. Books such as *Harawikuna,* a book of poetry by

Building an Underrepresented Collection   23

Mauro Mamani in Quechua and Aymara; *Illariy*, a book of poetry in Quechua by Washington Córdova Huamán; and the short stories book *Musyarqaniñam wañunaykita*, also in Quechua, compiled by César Itier illustrates that some publications were written with a specific reader in mind. In a conversation with Quechua creator Irma Alvarez Ccoscco, a native language activist in computerized media from Haquira, in Peru's Apurímac region, Alvarez noted that her poem, "Kawsaq," in the Quechua language, was meant to be read by Quechua speakers only.[11]

Alvarez's self-determination in choosing the audience she wanted to reach invites librarians to question whether purchasing certain materials violates Indigenous authors' right to decide where their literary creations should be held. This situation might pose a dilemma and require introspection for librarians who wish to preserve Indigenous literature and provide free access. This matter is even more complicated because the acquisition window declines considerably once the item is out of publication. For librarians participating in revitalizing Indigenous languages, cultures, histories, and the creative output of Indigenous literature, acquiring, promoting, and preserving these literary works is one crucial path to support their posterity.

The second and third selection criteria are the literary genre and readers as a target group. Latin American literature is known for its poetry, chronicles, essays, short stories, and novels. Indigenous literature has expanded its poetry oeuvre to include oral poetry, chants, therapeutic folk poetry, and incantations. A book such as *Conjuros y Ebriedades: Cantos de Mujeres Mayas*, published by the Taller Leñateros, a collective run by Mayan artists, Amerindian and mestizos in Chiapas, Mexico, is a compilation of poems and incantations in Spanish and Tzotzil accompanied by lithographs. Moreover, Taller Leñateros has published artistic book productions made with sustainable materials (Past et al.).[12]

Similarly, personal narratives as oral autobiographies offer unique eyesight into the lives of individuals from Indigenous communities. The oral autobiography of Mazatec poet and shaman María Sabina is an example of oral transmission transformed into a printed book. Sabina, who only spoke the Mazatec language and did not read and write, collaborated with a Mazatec local fellow, Álvaro Estrada, to record what later would be published as *Vida* (Sabina XIII, 15). In *Vida*, Sabina recounts her life lived in extreme poverty in the Oaxacan mountain village of Huautla in Mexico as she discovers her calling as a shaman, using the sacred power of the language of the saint children (*Psilocybin* mushrooms) known as "the Flesh of God" (25, 28).

A library acquisition of a book such as the autobiography *Vida* is at the forefront of an Indigenous literature collection. This book highlights the importance of oral tradition for its firsthand account of Mazatec medicinal rituals and spiritual cosmovision interlaced with the realms of death, life, folk culture, and Roman Catholicism. Sabina invokes the Virgin Magdalene and the Virgin Guadalupe mixing this religious invocation with her espirituality as a shaman when she says: " ... I am the water that looks ... the wise woman in medicine ... the woman herbalist (Sabina 73). Thus, Sabina's words suggest how Indigenous ways of knowing are interwoven with Roman Catholic doctrine, a legacy of the practice of conversion of Indigenous people to Christianity. Library materials that intimately connect to Indigenous oral tradition support curricula that depart from mainstream genres of literature to examine Indigenous knowledge from the viewpoint of Indigenous peoples.

Readers as a target group also affect purchasing decision-making, which is especially relevant when serving a particular academic department. Academic libraries with a youth collection should assess the ample representation of Indigenous children's picture books and short stories and have them available for students majoring in education. Future teachers might contemplate adding these books to their school curricula and integrating them as children learn about other cultures' traditions and ways of knowing. Books such as *Cuento del Conejo y el Coyote/Didxaguca' sti' Lexu ne Gueu'/Tale of the Rabbit and the Coyote*, in trilingual edition, Zapotec, Spanish, and English by Natalia Toledo; *Mä ancha suma anata ispira/Una Mágica Víspera de Carnaval: cuento Aymara* in bilingual edition Aymara Spanish by Carmen Muñoz Hurtado; and *Topilitzkuintli/El Perro Topil* in Nahuatl and Spanish by Elisa Ramírez Castañeda, display some of the topics covered in children's literature such as Indigenous mythology, folklore, legends, and festivities, etc. These books could be used in social studies units to familiarize students with Indigenous cultures from other regions of the American continent.

A fourth selection criterion is timeliness flexibility, which allows librarians to look retrospectively. To illustrate, let us consider currency when assessing the cuento (tale) *Kuya Kuya* by Óscar Colchado Lucio, initially published in 2007. This Andean love story is a must-have in academic libraries. Also available in a bilingual edition, Spanish and Quechua, *Kuya Kuya* represents a jewel of the Latin American literary genre cuento for adult readers, where Colchado integrates elements of the life of the Andean campesino with Indigenous folklore and romantic love. A retroactive approach to purchasing Indigenous materials ensures that librarians do not miss evaluating and purchasing important books of Indigenous literature published many years ago.

Building a Film Cinema Collection That Is Indigenous

Along the same line as Indigenous literature, there is a proliferation of audiovisual materials directed and produced by Indigenous and insider mestizo creators.[13] Film festivals such as Cine+Video Indígena (Chile),

Festival de Cine Latinoamericano en Lenguas Originarias (Peru), and Ficwallmapu Festival Internacional de Cine y las Artes Indigenas en Wallmapu (Chile) are some of the venues of propagation for Indigenous cinema that highlight feature films, short and long documentaries, and animations.[14] These moving pictures are of different lengths, thematic fluency, and expressive artistic composition, attesting not only to the creative output of Indigenous and racialized film creators but also to a desire to tell stories deeply connected to Indigenous communities from the point of view of Indigenous people.

Indigenous voices are documented through fictional stories, tales from the oral tradition, earthly and celestial landscapes connecting with the concept of cosmovision, and the voice of Indigenous and non-Indigenous insider creators. Anthropologist William Lempert distinguishes between insider and outsider models to differentiate between Indigenous films from ethnographic ones (Lempert). Indigenous filmmakers use their personal connections with Indigenous communities that translate in "critical indigenous identity narratives" as opposed to the outsider's perspective of ethnographers who are trained to analyze "cultural groups" (Lempert 23). Misak film director Luis Tróchez Tunubalá exposes the complexity and limitations of the outsider's view of the Indigenous that other Indigenous audiovisual creators probably share. In the documentary *Na misak*, Tróchez Tunubalá contrasts the tremendous cultural diversity found in Indigenous cultures with the perception of the Indigenous as inferior, uncivilized, and ignorant. This film director wonders why people see the Indigenous this way and, most remarkably, questions what is probably in the minds of Indigenous writers as well: "Am I less Indigenous if I practice the culture of the white men?" (Tróchez Tunubalá).

One impactful approach to Indigenous expression through audiovisual media is the animation and short documentary genres. These materials could be easily integrated into classroom engagement and critical thinking activities. To illustrate, the six-minute animation *Mapu Kufüll* by Mapuche director Seba Calfuqueo Aliste shows a young man whose grandmother has asked to gather mushrooms from the field. In the introductory lines, the narrator salutes, thanks, and asks the ngen of the wilshiko, "the *ngen* of the land and creator of the soil" (spirits from nature that live in the stream and that provide and protect), to help him in his quest. The animation, set to contrasting blue and shades of green colors depicting the water and forest, respectively, infuses spectators with a sense of serenity and appreciation for land conservation as though the viewers are connecting with this forest and its resources. The notion of conservation is demonstrated as the main character walks the woods, cuts a mushroom for his basket, and invariably ensures he dresses the dirt so the mushroom will sprout again. The story is told on

Mapudungun with English and Spanish subtitles to help people understand the storyline.

In subsequent chapters, we refer to Indigenous film as a pedagogical tool in newly conceived non-hegemonic curricula. University libraries supporting these curricula could aim to build a collection development workflow that sustains the acquisition of Indigenous cinema. One critical step in this workflow is remembering that acquiring these films could be as challenging as acquiring Indigenous literature. Thus, understanding what distinguishes Indigenous cinema from other types of films is of the essence. Consider that the nuances this chapter noted for acquiring Indigenous literature also apply to Indigenous cinema. While having Indigenous directors and producers behind Indigenous cinema productions is an attribute one could look for, it is expected to find mestizo and even people from other ancestry, with insider knowledge, involved in the creative and production team. These films could be spoken entirely in an Indigenous language, as a primarily driven force where language is a central component of the film, or have Indigenous terms and dialogues intersperse with the main narrative in a dominant language. Regarding the correlation between Spanish and Indigenous languages in cinematic productions within the regions of Latin America, although utilizing an Indigenous language is crucial for denoting cultural identity, Indigenous cinema appears to reconcile with utilizing the Spanish language as well.

Less ambiguity is found in the thematic lens, control over representation, and the insider voices supporting Indigenous films, critical elements to consider when building a collection of Indigenous cinema. Again, distinguishing between the prepositions *by/with* and *about* may clarify a librarian's questions about a film. No matter how insightful an ethnographic film is about an Indigenous community, if this film conceives Indigenous people as the subject of study and not the ones in control of their stories, this film could not be Indigenous in nature. Comparing how Indigenous and ethnographic films differ, Lempert notes that ethnographers focus on "cultural groups" from an "outsider's perspective." In contrast, the Indigenous filmmaker has a relationship with the community that fosters a "critical Indigenous identity" narrative (Lempert 23).[15]

Even following anthropological methodologies for filming, foreign ethnographic filmmakers may be tethered to colonialistic "biases and preconceptions" that lead them to "see and say anything about another culture from an insider's point of view" (Ash 103, Lempert 25).[16] This "outsider status" also halts many ethnographic films from truly representing an Indigenous culture as it would be represented "and experience from members of that culture" (Ash 23). Referring to the Yanomami people of Venezuela, ethnographic filmmaker Timothy Asch, who, in 1968, was creating records of the Yanomamo culture, stated in 1991:

While the making of a film that would depict how the Yanomami are living today seems to me to be an important and worthwhile venture, I am no longer as interested in making films about them as I am in seeing the kinds of films that they might make about themselves. Moreover, I now question my role as an outsider representing their life and concerns to the wider world. (102)

Ash acknowledged that it was important for the outside world to learn about and appreciate Indigenous communities and that cinematic communication was a much more potent tool than the spoken and written word to achieve intercultural communication (102). This filmmaker also granted that, as outsiders, foreign anthropologists sought to "understand and represent" Indigenous cultures, likely providing a different take on a given culture than the one an insider could provide (103). Nonetheless, an outsider's representation might always be missing a significant point or a matter of identity or cultural importance that could only be expressed by an insider's voice. When it comes to control over representation, it is "time for them [Indigenous people] to tell their stories in their own ways. And it is important for us to listen" (Ash 106).

The selection criteria presented above will assist librarians in the acquisition process of Indigenous cinema, especially when these films may be a part of a class's curriculum. However, while curricula could offer a structured space for exploring Indigenous cultures through cinema, there are other instances in which Indigenous cinema could be a part of academia. For example, higher education could welcome Indigenous films in festivals organized by a university's study centers, programs, and members from academic units. A critical matter for academic libraries concerning the purchase of films outside the confines of streaming video databases is determining when public performance rights (PPR) should be acquired and what type of license is required to protect Indigenous film copyrights.

Faculty might be under the impression that because a material (such as a film) is used for educational purposes, its use is always protected under the fair use doctrine. This belief is flawed. Besides films in the public domain, which are not subjected to copyright laws in the United States, the legal doctrine of fair use allows the "unlicensed use" of copyrighted materials for research, teaching, criticism, etc., under section 107 of the Copyright Act, which states the four factors that should be considered when applying fair use:

1 The purpose and character of the use, including whether such use is of a commercial nature or is for non-profit educational purposes.
2 The nature of the copyrighted work.

3 The amount and substantiality of the portion used in relation to the copyrighted work as a whole.
4 The effect of the use upon the potential market for or value of the copyrighted work. (*U.S. Copyright Office Fair Use Index*)[17]

Noticeably, the purpose of showing a film in the classroom, where the audience is students enrolled in the given course, should align with the curricular goals of the course. Nonetheless, not all educational purposes are covered by the doctrine of fair use, or the TEACH Act (Technology, Education, and Copyright Harmonization Act, S. 487). According to the U.S. Senate Committee on the Judiciary's analysis of the bill on virtual classes, Section 110(2) (A) of the TEACH Act

> ... the bill requires that the transmission be made "by or at the direction of an instructor as an integral part of a class session." In sum, the work must be used as an integral part of a classroom experience (albeit a virtual one), controlled by the instructor, rather than as supplemental or background information to be experienced independently. (Senate Committee on the Judiciary)[18]

Therefore, linking a film to the course's learning management system may or may not be protected, depending on the educational goals of the course and the use of this film. To the surprise of many faculty, showing films in festivals organized within a university campus, even when free, is not typically considered fair use. For this type of viewing, PPR should be purchased to have permission to show the film. The idea behind PPR is to obtain rights and respect the copyright holder's intellectual property. In my experience, I have seen faculty acquiring verbal or written (via email) consent from the copyright holder to show an Indigenous film at a festival. Securing this permission enables libraries to provide lawful access to the film.

University libraries have a responsibility to procure PPR every time is needed and, in particular, librarians who are in direct contact with faculty could educate them about the importance of purchasing film licenses to uphold copyright laws. Nonetheless, it is not just a matter of legal compliance but also a matter of ethical acquisition practices and collection use. Indigenous film productions, which tend to have limited budgets, could be exploited unintentionally when these films are exhibited in academic-organized festivals without proper licenses. Although unintentional exploitation does not convey a deliberated state of mind to abuse, exploitation is a particularly sensitive issue for Indigenous communities who have been victims of exploitative practices for centuries.

Beyond the Political Divide

Apart from the selection criteria addressed, a matter that deserves attention when building an Indigenous literature and film collection is the content itself, especially for informational books of analysis, criticism, and interpretation concentrating on societal issues affecting Indigenous communities. Because some of the Indigenous film and literature works tend to present socio-geo-political narratives that align with progressive ideologies, some might argue against content that takes people out of their comfort zone, presenting realities that some people and institutions dispute. Daniel Heath Justice notes that if we only see what is familiar and comfortable, then literature becomes a "mirror," not a "window" where we engage with the world and are part of a bigger context (Hanson 119).

When grievances on wokeness and overdrive book censoring are at the center stage of socio-political narratives, controversial content may deter some academic libraries from diverging funds to purchase Indigenous film and literature, even in the name of research and knowledge. This situation may be especially noticeable in universities where curricula and faculty research do not support this acquisition. This matter was raised to me in a panel I presented at the Seminar on the Acquisition of Latin American Library Materials (SALALM) in June 2023. The American Library Association recommends that academic librarians look at materials that "represent a variety of perspectives and controversial subjects" and support instruction and research.[19] Indigenous film and literature usually cover a non-hegemonic perspective and may require librarians to assess materials highlighting controversial topics such as cultural sovereignty, land exploitation, force assimilation, etc. Therefore, one approach to developing an Indigenous film and literature collection is to look beyond the political divide to appreciate these works from their literary, creative, historical, and Indigenous knowledge-based value.

As stated above, a thoughtful attitude is required to advocate for revitalizing Indigenous languages and cultures through film and literature, which necessitates looking beyond political affiliations. Although people probably have political preferences in academia, acquiring knowledge should be above affiliations. To illustrate, a Buddhist person accepts the precepts of Buddha, but this belief should not stop this person from learning about Judaism or any other religion. Different types of knowledge support an exhaustive understanding of the world around us. For members of higher education institutions, this comprehensive mindset fosters the path to value Indigenous wisdom passed through its literary and cinematographic output.

As I have indicated, applying divergent selection criteria for selecting and purchasing Indigenous film and literature is necessary when building a collection. Examining the book industry and interprofessional collaborations are the next helpful steps to finding underrepresented materials and providing access.

Exploring the Book and Library's Market Trade

Library customers are probably unfamiliar with the book acquisition process rushing, behind library doors. For a library in the United States, ordering a book (firm orders) through Amazon is a straightforward customer-digital interface interaction. However, when ordering books from Latin America, this process requires partnerships, communication with international book vendors, and relationships with authors and publishing houses. In the article "Managing Customer Relationships: A Book Vendor Point-of-View," George Coe notes the complicated library's workflow that relies on "contractual arrangements" with book vendors in what is known as approval plans (44). I will refer to these contracts and interprofessional relationships promptly. Still, I wanted to emphasize that understanding the book industry and the academic library's marketplace for print books is essential when trying to find who publishes and sells Indigenous literature.

There are several stakeholders involved in the book business apart from publishers. Authors, distributors, book wholesalers, libreros (book vendors), book retailers (bookstores), and librarians, not to mention those involved in getting books into the hands of readers. Book wholesalers, such as Baker & Taylor, buy books from publishers and self-published authors and sell these books to bookstores, online retailers (Amazon and Barnes & Noble), and libraries (Collins, *The Write Way* 18–29).[20] Book distributors work for publishers and also sell books to bookstores while offering multifaceted services such as placing books into the market, warehousing, and shipping (Collins *The Write Way* 16–17).[21]

Large commercial publishers do not usually receive manuscripts directly from an author; instead, they rely on editors who contact agents to select a book, edit it, and prepare it for publication ("How Publishing Works"). The smaller independent publishers receive manuscripts from writers, theoretically opening doors to authors of Indigenous literature and providing information of great value for librarians who must connect with these publishers to purchase Indigenous literature. Trade publishers of fiction and non-fiction literature may also allow authors to submit online submissions, and sometimes mainstream publishers have imprints that support manuscripts submitted with Indigenous-focused stories. For example, Heartdrum, an imprint for HarperCollins, invites Indigenous writers and illustrators from the United States and Canada to submit stories for children and young adult literature ("Services, Sales & Rights").

This information is relevant for those trying to build an Indigenous literature collection. While renowned Indigenous authors may publish in large, multinational publishing companies, the small, alternative, or non-traditional publishing house may take the work of emerging and lesser-known Indigenous authors. I referred to this topic in a 2020 study that examined the representation of Hispano-American presses in 88 university libraries in the United States (Ibacache et al.). When trying to locate Indigenous literature, it is helpful to understand the book industry and know who publishes Indigenous books and what genre these publishers support.

On many occasions, Indigenous literature is published by fondos culturales (government funds set aside for cultural projects and publications), such as the Fondo de Cultura Económica in Mexico, Fondo Editorial del Congreso de la República in Peru, and the Fondo Editorial del Instituto Estatal de Educación Pública de Oaxaca. Other publishers include the Centro de Estudios Interculturales e Indígenas in Chile, and university presses such as the Universidad Nacional Mayor de San Marcos, a significant publisher for Indigenous literature in Peru. Peru is one country with a generous landscape of editoriales that publishes Indigenous authors and works in Indigenous languages.[22]

Learning about these publishing houses, their mission, and whether they support Indigenous literature is paramount to finding these books, which are often hard to find. Diversifying book-finding practices and selection to include non-mainstream editoriales that carry Indigenous literature also balances the book industry, which is driven by multinationals' market domination. To illustrate, the Chilean publishing house *Pehuén Editores* began as a publishing center of political resistance in the 1980s. Now *Pehuén Editores* emphasizes its connection with a literary production that seeks to preserve the memory of the Indigenous nations and the cultural and historical patrimony of the country ("¿Quiénes somos?").[23] As you can see, mapping editoriales that offer Indigenous literature is a valuable collection development strategy to support purchasing pathways. The next step for libraries to find these books is communication and interprofessional collaboration with stakeholders, including authors. Through this network of connections, libraries could secure access, making books openly available via print or digital format.

Interprofessional Collaboration: Facilitating the Participation of Indigenous Authors in the Conversation

Collection development in libraries typically does not include direct communication with authors. University libraries purchase print books through contracts with international and national book vendors, where these vendors send shipments with many books following the contract's specifications (approval plans). Book purchases are also made through one-time orders directly from retailers like Amazon, bookstores, and publishers. Some of these publishers offer print and electronic books (e-books) for the university market, and library vendors such as ProQuest provide print and e-books that librarians may select from an online ordering system. None of these transactions require interactions with an author. However, Indigenous literature from Latin America is a book market not easily found in mainstream book market venues, and acquaintances with authors and communication with libreros could demonstrate a reciprocal beneficial relationship.

Finding emerging authors, Indigenous works of literature, and the editoriales that publish this work is challenging and, at the same time, inspiring. A network of relationships with authors, libreros, publishers, and various book fairs promoting Indigenous literature opens doors of discovery for this distinct literature that defies the saturated book topics available to the public. Interprofessional collaboration with these stakeholders broadens collection development strategies and facilitates Indigenous authors' participation in the library book-purchasing market. Additionally, connecting with the creators of Indigenous literature helps us visualize a decolonial approach to building a collection. Silvia Rivera Cusicanqui, examining the meaning of decolonization, poses the question of how we can change the "exclusive ethnographic we" that presents Indigenous people as the focus of study for the "inclusive we" that positions Indigenous people as equals (Rivera Cusicanqui 97).

Interprofessional outreach to authors and non-mainstream publishers requires inventiveness and audacity, especially when finding authors and publishers in interactive technologies such as social media. For example, Fabiola Carrillo Tieco is a Nahuatl author who periodically promotes Indigenous books on Facebook, propelled by author-driven promotion in social media.[24] Social media is a helpful digital space for librarians and libreros trying to find authors and learn about their new publications and those of their peers, especially if these publications are self-published (Clark and Phillips 95).[25] Similarly, the Universidad Nacional Autónoma de México (UNAM)'s Facebook page, *Libros UNAM*, also features news related to its academic publishing, *Publicaciones Fomento Editorial*, which offers the Premio de Cuento Joven UNAM-SECTEI. This competition invites high school students from Mexico to submit tales in Spanish or an Indigenous language (*Convocatoria Premio Cuento Joven UNAM-SECTEI 2023*).

For *libreros* and librarians, connection with authors, news of literary competitions, and social media accounts promoting Indigenous literature, for example, are relevant to finding young, talented writers and those who are self-promoting their titles. Yet, while locating Indigenous literature, their authors, and editoriales that publish it is crucial, this work could harvest much more symbiotically beneficial relationships if these stakeholders embrace meaningful communication. It is paramount that librarians and book vendors communicate collection development needs and the strategies to fulfill them, respectively. Whether a librarian or a book vendor, in an acquisition relationship, learns of authors, editoriales, or other book vendors who offer Indigenous literature, sharing this information may facilitate the purchase process and henceforth access.

Consequently, for a *librero* procuring books from Mexico, communicating with Publicaciones UNAM to purchase the anthology containing the works of the winner of the UNAM-SECTEI competition opens an opportunity to advance emerging authors and to help academic libraries provide access to Indigenous literature written by young authors. Promoting these interactions among authors, publishers, librarians, and libreros requires intentional need-based communication. Sam Brooks, an executive at EBSCO, referring to infrastructure and software vendors, wrote, "In essence, open lines of communication and the basic sharing of information is at the core of library/vendor relations" (2). Brooks emphasized that vendors and librarians could learn from each other to serve constituencies better and that a crucial aspect of this relationship was the "understanding of needs" (2, 4).

For librarians building an Indigenous literature collection and relying on approval plans as a formal venue to receive books, dependence on libreros to access Indigenous authors and literature published in various countries from Latin America necessitates a need-based interprofessional communication.[26] In a need-based interprofessional communication, librarians ensure feedback about their book needs, which is especially critical if approval plans do not specify Indigenous literature. Moreover, sharing with libreros what publishers carry Indigenous literature in the countries they cover or what Indigenous authors are resonating in social networking sites informs libreros of specific needs related to this literature. This two-way communication is the backbone of acquiring Indigenous literature and providing access.

Another network of connections may be constructed in conferences and ferias del libro (book fairs) that focus on Indigenous literature. The Latin and Latinx Studies Center at the University of Colorado Boulder has organized two 1-week in-person and virtual conferences called Celebrating the Indigenous Americas in 2021 and 2022. In these celebrations, educators, artists, activists, scholars, and authors shared Indigenous knowledge in various subjects. Engaging directly with authors could inform librarians of an author's creative process, thematic inspiration, and relevance for the higher education classroom. These events were sponsored by the Latin American and Latinx Studies Center, the U.S. Department of Education, Title VI IFLE (International and

Foreign Language Education), the Center for Native and Indigenous Studies, University Libraries, the American Music Research Center, and Department of Women and Gender Studies.

Although attending book fairs demands international travel funds, these fairs offer opportunities for building interprofessional relationships and collaborations among librarians, libreros, and the many publishers, authors, and literary agents that attend. To illustrate, in 2023, the Centro de Estudios sobre Pueblos Originarios of the Biblioteca Nacional de la República Argentina, a body of the Argentinian Ministerio de Cultura (Department of Culture), invited editoriales that offer Indigenous literature to participate in the Feria del Libro sobre Pueblos Originarios ("Convocatoria para la Feria del Libro sobre Pueblos Originarios"). Similarly, the city of Osorno in Chile launched its first Feria del Libro Mapuche Williche to promote Mapuche authors in June 2023, and the Municipio de Oaxaca in Mexico also launched the Feria Regional de Libro en Lenguas Indigenas in 2022 (Valdebenito).[27] These book fairs highlight a movement to appreciate Indigenous literature and provide a place to socialize and build interprofessional connections.

Building a collection of Indigenous literature and film necessitates reliance on different selection criteria to inform the assessment, selection, and acquisition process. These criteria depart from conventional selection guidance but are paramount to considering this literature comprehensively. Additionally, through interprofessional collaboration, various stakeholders participate in the power of healing as a frame to foster alliances between Indigenous and non-Indigenous people. This symbiotic interprofessional relationship is crucial in acquiring and building communication bridges among authors, publishers, *libreros*, and libraries. If we consider Indigenous materials a gift to connect with Indigenous ways of knowing, this collection development approach supports this film and literature's creative and interconnected output, facilitates the materials for the creation of a non-hegemonic curriculum, and broadens students' access to materials that connect them to Indigenous knowledge.

Notes

1 Through this program, members from the university and the broader community may submit purchase suggestions that are received and assessed by librarians. Once a suggestion is evaluated and approved, the item is ordered and joins the collection.
2 There are several types of collections in a library comprising books, audiovisuals, databases, etc. However, each one of these collections could also be divided into collections that could be organized by topic, format (print, electronic), type of book (oversized, miniature, cartonera books), genre, etc. For example, an Indigenous literature collection is one type of collection.

3 Kimmerer refers to the "home of our non-human kinfolk," alluding to all the animals and plants that live in Native peoples' homeland (17).
4 Kimmerer refers to the human relationship to strawberries (29–30).
5 See "Gift-giving Practices," The Minnesota Historical Society.
6 For an explanation of racialization of Indigenous peoples, see the Introduction.
7 Andrea Echeverría notes that Aniñir's poetry admits the "existence of a new urban Mapuche" born in the capital of Chile, outside ancestral Mapuche lands, whose identity intertwines with that of the rural Mapuche and thus counter "historical stereotypes" that assign the Mapuche people an identity associated with rural Indigenous living in the south of Chile ("Mapurbe Identity and Admapu in David Aniñir's Poetry" 209–18).
8 Marisol de la Cadena argues that semantically, the term mestizo has more connotations than the mixture of Spaniards and Indigenous and classifications based on "purity of blood." Indian caciques marrying "tributary Indian women" were also considered mestizo, and people with similar racial marks could self-identify themselves differently (264). In contemporary times, biological, cultural, wealth, and class features prompt people's self-identification attesting to a "semantic instability" of the term.
9 See also Echeverría, "Mapurbe Identity and Admapu in David Aniñir's Poetry," 212.
10 Yeisi Julieth Niño refers to the book of poetry *Walinto,* which is translated from Spanish to Mapudungun, as a bridge of communication between these two cultures (93).
11 In a conversation with Álvarez Ccoscco, this poet explained that publishing her poetry in bilingual editions was not her priority; she intended to write for the Quechua reader (Álvarez Ccoscco, "Poetry Reading"). See a recording of the poem "Kuwaq" in *Musuq Illa* and the lecture "Bringing It Home 02" at the Smithsonian Institution.
12 See also "Sobre nosotrxs," *Taller Leñateros: Arte Maya Contemporáneo Sustentable.* https://tallerlenateros.com/qui%C3%A9nes-somos-1.
13 I borrow William Lempert's insider-outsider model to denote film creators that consider themselves Indigenous, but also those film directors that, although not Indigenous, have meaningfully experienced and lived with Indigenous communities.
14 The Museo Chileno de Arte Precolombino is hosting the Cine + Video Indigena in 2023, with films focusing on themes such as identity, ancestral knowledge, human rights, and the protection and defense of territories, among others: https://museo.precolombino.cl/cinevideo-2023/. The Festival de Cine Latinoamericano en Lenguas Originarias has an emphasis on Indigenous languages: https://www.festivalcinelenguasoriginarias.com/. Fillwapmapu was launched in 2015: https://www.ficwallmapu.cl/quienes-somos/.
15 Lempert compared two films with similar subject matter: Dustinn Craig's *4 Wheel War Pony* (2008), a short film, where members of the White Mountain Apache use a skateboard for footage, and Jerry Leach's ethnographic film *Trobriand Cricket* (1975).
16 I use the term foreign to denote ethnographic filmmakers and anthropologists who would be considered outsiders to an Indigenous community. The term foreign also suggests a separation from Indigenous ethnographers and anthropologists.
17 See also Limitations on Exclusive Rights: Fair Use. https://www.copyright.gov/title17/92chap1.html#107.
18 To read the whole analysis, see United States Senate 107th Congress, 1st Session https://www.copyright.gov/docs/regstat031301.html. The libguide

prepared by the George A. Smathers Libraries provides a friendly summary to understand when public performance rights are needed and the application of the TEACH Act in online classes. "Copyright on Campus: Showing Movies in Class and on Campus." https://guides.uflib.ufl.edu/copyright/video. I heartily thank Alexander Watkins, associate professor and art and architecture librarian at the University of Colorado Boulder, for explaining the difference between showing films as part of the course curriculum and streaming films where fair use will depend of the amount of the film students are required to watch, the context within the goals of the course, and the application of the doctrine of fair use.

19 The American Library Association provides guidance on selection criteria for different types of libraries, including academic library ("Selection Criteria").
20 Amy Collins is an agent with the Talcott Notch Literary Services agency.
21 See also Collins, "The Differences Between Book Wholesalers and Distributors."
22 Las casas editoras or editoriales are the Spanish terms for publishing houses. Some of these editoriales are Lluvia Editores, Pakarina Ediciones, Grupo Editorial Arteidea, Debate, Editorial Crecer, and PEISA.
23 Other book vendors and independent publishing houses that carry Indigenous literature are Abya Yala Editorial, librosperuanos.com, Pluralia Ediciones, Enhacore Books, F&G Editores, Editorial LOM, Editorial Ocho Libros, Editorial Pehuen, Editorial Trillas in Mexico, and Editorial Cuarto Propio.
24 Many authors need to prove they can sell their books, and successful self-promotion could pave the way for a book deal; see Collins, *The Write Way*, 9–11.
25 Giles Clark and Angus Phillips are referring to self-published e-books.
26 An approval plan is a book acquisition method where a contract is created with a profile stating the libraries' book needs.
27 See "Inauguran la Feria Regional del Libro en Lenguas Indígenas (FERELLI 2022)," *La Onda Oaxaca*.

2 Universities' Libraries as More Than Repositories of Information

Kathia Ibacache

We all probably have a preconceived idea of what an academic library is or does. The American Library Association defines academic libraries as those that "serve colleges and universities, their students and faculty," providing subject expertise to the multiple schools, departments, centers, and colleges that are part of higher education institutions ("Academic Libraries"). One of university libraries' most consequential services in the United States is access to their collections. Some librarians are tasked with collection development responsibilities in any academic library. These librarians work to satisfy constituents' multilayered needs. One of these librarians is the subject liaison, who interfaces with subject-specific academic units, focusing on faculty and students' curricular and research needs and addressing gaps of relevance in the collection.

As subject liaisons prioritize these needs, they can ideally support all their constituents, depending on the available budget. However, what happens when academic libraries' collections lack materials created by minorities or are outside the canon? Or what happens when faculty offer courses using materials that only represent the dominant culture? When selecting and acquiring materials, could subject liaisons go beyond what current curricula or research require and select works not yet recognized by academia? Could these librarians become cultural brokers?

In this chapter, we will reflect on these questions and argue that subject liaisons could mobilize acquisition practices that are not limited to mirroring curricular needs and could open a window into new forms of knowledge that do not simply reflect the dominant culture. In making this argument, we will examine ways to improve the discoverability of Indigenous literature through bibliographic enhancement data (BIBED), which can provide a bridge to connect students and faculty to these underrepresented works of literature. We then show how Indigenous literature, especially when published in multilingual editions, can play a role in developing students' cultural

DOI: 10.4324/9781032660561-3

consciousness. We conclude by juxtaposing the presence of print and digital books, noting that while digitizing Indigenous books is vital for access in emergency lockdowns, maintaining the print book market is much needed to balance the representation of Indigenous works in canon-heavy built collections.

Academic Librarians as Cultural Brokers

Mary Ann Jezewski defined culture brokering "as the act of bridging, linking, or mediating between groups or persons for the purpose of reducing conflict or producing change" (497). Jezewski was referring to a process that facilitated health care for migrant farmworkers. Nevertheless, the concept of cultural brokers has been around for centuries, with anthropologists defining it as those who act as "middlemen" or "negotiators" (National Center for Cultural Competence 2).[1] Anthropologist Eric Wolf took up the concept of "broker" in 1956 to refer to people who mediated between different social groups in Mexican society (1076). Wolf's brokers acted like "buffers," advocating for the interests of the groups. Indeed, anthropology scholars have connected the cultural brokers' functionality to one that "bridges gaps" (Jezewski 498).

We borrow the notions of the intermediary and the one that bridges the gap to associate the subject librarian with collection development responsibilities to a cultural broker. In this role, the librarian connects students and faculty to underrepresented materials, especially Indigenous books and audiovisual materials, and provides resources that may loosen complete dependency on a canon representing only the dominant society. As cultural brokers, librarians have two roles: 1) they work as a bridge (or a facilitator) that connects students and faculty with Indigenous literature, films, and other materials, and 2) they act as advocates for students' development of transcultural skills.

As cultural brokers in the role of the facilitator, liaison librarians are a bridge among students, faculty, the material itself, the book vendor, and the library that provides access. In this role, the cultural broker librarian communicates a need in the collection to acquisition colleagues and vendors to acquire underrepresented materials and provide access. The liaison librarian utilizes a window framework for acquisition, opening paths to purchase materials that provide access to the literary and creative works of people representing different cultures worldwide, even when these works are not part of the canon. The metaphor of the window that opens acquisition to materials from culturally diverse creators juxtaposes that of the mirror, which follows acquisition practices that only reflect tangible canon-based curricular needs. Naturally, fulfilling concrete curricular and research needs is at the core of duties, a responsibility academic librarians follow at heart.

However, a cultural broker librarian bridging material needs and access goes further, detecting gaps in the collection and even in curricular offerings about topics of societal importance that may be connected to groups outside the dominant culture.

Librarian John J. Doherty, examining the literary canon as a mirror of elitism and a dominant parameter for authority, notes that the canon's "exclusionary nature" will probably miss works of literature of relevance and will be unable to represent the whole society (404). Fortunately, Doherty notes that canons can also evolve and that librarians could serve as "facilitators of exploration" by acquiring underrepresented materials and thus be a part of the transformation of the canon (404). It is librarians' participation in an evolving canon that Doherty sees as their "true historical responsibility," progressing from merely collecting to engaging in collection development, an approach to acquisition that should consider non-canonical works (404). Although Doherty does not refer to librarians as brokers, this author suggests that academic librarians are responsible for facilitating the purchase of materials outside the traditional canon as these librarians have "an obligation to the future" (405).

As a facilitator, once a cultural broker librarian has located a gap for underrepresented materials, the librarian will communicate this need to vendors and others in the acquisition team. This librarian will also need to allocate funds to bridge the gap. The intersection between an underrepresented material and its recipients (faculty and students) is where cultural brokers create a connection or bridge. Their role is to mediate between the material's creator, the book vendor or distributor, and the library that provides access to advance the acquisition conversation when possible or necessary.

The second role of the cultural broker librarian is that of an advocator for students' development of transcultural skills, providing access to accomplished books by Indigenous authors in multilingual editions. Materials in bilingual and trilingual editions with translations students can read allow them to understand the content and grasp that languages represent a variety of cultures in the world, including Indigenous cultures. These materials may particularly impact monolingual students who, for any reason, are unaware of cultures outside their own. How many of us are abreast of the Miskito people and their language? Or that there are more than 4,000 Indigenous languages of the nearly 6,700 languages of the world, thus representing about 4,000 cultures if we consider that each language is an aperture to the cultural landscape of a specific nation ("Permanent Forum on Indigenous Issues").

Multilingual materials also open windows to all students, including plurilingual students, when encountering words or expressions in other languages that express thoughts or ideas more accurately than their mother tongue (Breuer and Van Steendam 1). Because languages attest to the cultural expression of a nation, their stories, and their ways of knowing, students' access to these materials or having them integrated as part of the curriculum in a class enhances their potential to develop transcultural skills. These skills, understood as the ability to value different cultural perspectives, are competencies that could be built when readers have access to Indigenous knowledge and creative works by other cultures.[2]

As a bridge, the cultural broker librarian could share new additions to the collection with faculty so that these materials could be of interest for specific curricular offerings or the development of a new societal-connected course. This proactive action entails the broker librarian being knowledgeable of the courses available to students and matching underrepresented materials according to the topic of these courses. Naturally, faculty will create syllabi and select course materials at their discretion. Still, when the cultural broker librarian communicates the purchases of underrepresented materials of literary value and interest to faculty, these titles could hopefully ignite curiosity, assessment, and their addition to future courses.

We invoke advocacy relating to the curriculum, not wishing for librarians to breach into the work of faculty but as a way of facilitating students' development of cultural consciousness. This would be accomplished through books representing multiple ways of knowing as passed on by Indigenous wisdom. As a cultural broker, the liaison librarian should surpass the neutrality associated with librarians who try to convey a pluralistic society in the collection by purchasing materials mainly published by large publishing houses. Librarian specialist Paul Thomas discusses the neutrality issue when librarians try to represent a pluralistic society with acquisition practices based on purchasing materials mainly published by mainstream large publishing houses. This monopoly-based transaction defeats the notion of a "balanced collection," as these publishers are likely to "promote the hegemonic ideology that keeps them in power" (Thomas 4). Indigenous literature truly offers an outreach opportunity for the broker librarian to reach out to non-mainstream publishers like those who publish experimental and non-traditional literature and Indigenous authors and even create connections among these stakeholders.

Referring to a hybrid mental health therapy approach that combines Indigenous knowledge and Western therapeutic approaches for refugees and the role of cultural brokers, E. Anne Marshall notes that brokers "can help transform systems and institutions to be more open and flexible about cultural diversity" (288). For higher education institutions to reach a transformation point that is more open to non-hegemonic curricular initiatives, they could start by supporting the creation of courses that use underrepresented materials of academic and cultural value. In this transformational setting, the broker librarian could be crucial in supporting these courses.

In this instance, it is the role of the cultural broker librarian to open acquisition practices to be more welcoming of cultural diversity, thus impacting the character of academic libraries from one that works as a repository of works by the dominant society to one that is connected to evolving societal needs and practices through inclusive collection development. To be aware and proactive of these evolving needs, subject librarians would have to defy university libraries' reputation as continuators of hegemonic discourses in education.[3] Opening acquisition practices to acquire multilingual materials representing different ways of knowing offers an opportunity to balance and renovate constructs in higher education and within the institutional habitus of an academic library.[4]

Discovering Indigenous Collections

I have argued that the subject librarian could be a cultural broker to provide access to underrepresented materials, specifically Indigenous literature. Once these materials arrive at a library, their discoverability in library catalogs will enhance constituents' ability to find them. Typically, what makes an item (book, article, audiovisual materials, and other library holdings) discoverable in library catalogs depends on multiple variables, from metadata elements, search algorithms, indexing, and even the search terms people use to find an item.

Searching behaviors or how we interact with search engines are complicated, even for information professionals like librarians. For example, one of my colleagues was looking for the film *Mothers of the Land* in the University of Colorado Boulder's library catalog and could not find it under this name. They knew the film's original language was Spanish and Quechua, so they went to Google, found its Spanish name, *Sembradoras de Vida*, and used it in the search. When the film appeared in the library catalog after the first search failed, my colleague noticed that the English name was also in the record, yet the first search had not produced a successful response. These librarians had to modify their search and use different search terms on the second search try. Many students and faculty have likely felt frustrated at one point or another by a failed search in an academic library catalog; I encountered many of those when looking for unknown items (not known titles), especially materials in Indigenous languages. Given this, how can libraries make books in Indigenous languages more easily discoverable or promote Indigenous materials in library catalogs?

Inspiration might be drawn from multiple Internet-based social bibliographic commercial and networking sites. Academic library catalog users are probably familiar with sites such as Amazon, LibraryThing,

Common Sense Media, Goodreads, and Barnes and Noble. These users might even think searching for books in library catalogs is as simple as doing a Google search. Their thinking is not unreasonable; Google relies on a computational technology called natural language processing *(NLP)*. This allows computers to understand human language, allowing this Internet search engine to understand users' questions and match responses closely; "it feels like our results are customized by someone who knows us" (Q.ai-Powering a Personal Wealth Movement). However, searching university library catalogs provides an entirely different experience, as NLP typically does not support these catalogs.

Because users looking for books in Indigenous languages may rely on other types of information such as table of contents, summaries, and user-generated data such as reviews and tags, one way to respond to these needs is to include bibliographic enhancement data (BIBED) in academic library catalogs. BIBED are links to external bibliographic data, such as summaries, abstracts, book covers, reviews, ratings, tags, metrics, and content notes. Shuheng Wu referred to BIBED as "additions to traditional library catalogs" that help users find desired titles, evaluate them, find related resources, and even allow collaboration (309). In 2008, the Library of Congress Working Group on the Future of Bibliographic Control advised that bibliographic control should welcome "all library materials, diverse community of users, and a multiplicity of venues where information is sought" (Library of Congress Working Group 10).

The university library catalog could strive to connect with those multiple digital bibliographic environments where users seek information. This connection would benefit patrons looking for titles; as the aforementioned working group noted: "bibliographic control is increasingly a matter of managing relationships" with environments such as Amazon, Google, WorldCat, and Wikipedia, for example (Library of Congress Working Group 10). The matter should not be as much about what patrons need to customize bibliographic records since these needs vary greatly but what searching behaviors and search terminology users utilize (Hoffman 637).[5] Financial distress, time constraints, and staff shortcuts aside, in a perfect world, the academic library catalog should connect with other web-based bibliographic environments to create links, add data from other bibliographic environments into records, and, most importantly, create a collaborative network for bibliographic data sharing with the broad academic library community. The Library of Congress Working Group on the Future of Bibliographic Control highlights these collaborative actions as "key to the future success of libraries" (11).

Many libraries already rely on the bibliographic information provided by the Library of Congress and OCLC Connexion; should branching out to social bibliographic sites and weaving BIBED into library catalogs be commonplace, this kinship could offer users a familiar and user-connected searching experience. Wu noted that BIBED enhances users' searching experience as they evaluate, locate specific titles, discover related items, and increase subject access and users' participation and collaboration (309). Promoting related items is critical for users to learn about and connect with other Indigenous works of literature. Through this helpful feature, users may navigate to other books that offer similar topics or additional works by the same author.

How BIBED enhances the searching experience of someone looking for Indigenous books could be argued from the user's viewpoint. Suppose one considers the bibliographic data contained in LibraryThing for the book *Braiding Sweetgrass*. In that case, we will find various tags (botany, ecology, environment, Native Americans, plants, science …) linking readers to related titles, members' recommendations and reviews, additional fields for genre, popular book covers for this title, and even its Library of Congress and Melvil Decimal System classification. Lawson and Voorbij noted that tags used by LibraryThing correlated better to the natural language used by people in searches than the controlled metadata included in subject headings (qtd. in Bogers and Petras 16). Similarly, by examining the same title on Amazon, another social cataloging site, we will find reviews from professional organizations and journalists, bibliographic data on product details, and highlights from Kindle readers. These sites provide data points and an interface that connects with users wishing to evaluate what they find, discover other topical-related books, find tags or keywords associated with titles, and relate to other readers. BIBED could provide a multi-layered interaction between the user and the library catalog, these sites, and other readers' tags, reviews, and summaries.

Enhancing academic library catalog records with bibliographic data from social bibliographic sites may help users interact with library catalogs in the same familiar way they do on these sites. For example, consider a general search where a patron is looking for a bilingual poetry book in Zapotec and English but does not know the name of an author or the title of a book. The search terms will probably include the keywords "poetry," "Zapotec," and "English," or "Zapotec poetry" and "English translation." For this patron to be able to find in the library catalog any book of poetry in Zapotec and English, the access points for records for bilingual poetry books in these two languages would need to include, as a minimum, the language of the book (Zapotec/English) and hopefully the subject (Zapotec poetry). The lack of this fundamental information in unknown-item searches where the author and the title are unspecified will make bibliographic records for Zapotec poetry books with English translations undiscoverable.

BIBED could also facilitate searches by connecting with users' preferred search terms. If data points indexed in library catalogs are inadequate or not in sync with users' selected search terms, search results might be defective. Similarly, if subject headings related to Indigenous people are not updated to move away from colonialist descriptions, patrons who utilize non-settler language in their searches will likely encounter failed searches. Several Library and Information Science (LIS) researchers have addressed the issue of colonialist terminology. Karl Petit and Erin Elzi referred to offensively controlled vocabulary in the Library of Congress subject headings. These authors suggested working at the local library level to address this issue and include accurate cultural representation of Indigenous Nations in library catalogs (Petit and Elzi).

Take, for example, the bilingual Zapotec poetry book mentioned above. If its library catalog record describes its author as "Indians of North America," a currently seen pejorative and generalized phrase to describe dozens of Indigenous Nations in North America, a patron utilizing the search term "Zapotec people," terminology that represents Zapotec authors, will not find it. Special collections cataloging librarian Elizabeth Hobert notes issues around vocabularies that MARC 21 records contain by relying on "settler" terminologies and not including the names of tribes to "describe Indigenous people" (Hobart 60).

Hobert examines the "choice of terms" and controlled vocabulary to describe Native American authors in the MARC 21 field 386, where catalogers can enter demographic information for authors and contributors in this field (60). Settler terminologies used in records tend to think of Indigenous people as "something from the past," with derogatory and generic language that departs from the concept of identity, which resonates considerably with Indigenous people in the present. Hobert exemplifies this problem by recounting a branch librarian's experience trying to help Musqueam patrons find materials at a time when bibliographic records omit the term Musqueam and described these materials as "Coast Salish Indians."[6]

Improving discoverability for Indigenous collections is a matter that has been on my mind since trying to locate the name of a trilingual book of poetry that contained a particular poem a few years ago. I had the poem's name and the author but not the book's title or the publisher. We imagine students and faculty having similar issues when they only have a few pieces of the puzzle. Should BIBED help with the discoverability of materials in Indigenous languages, subject liaisons could work with catalogers to ensure that meaningful data is linked and indexed in bibliographic records. We should consider collaboration among catalogers and liaisons as an asset to facilitate discoverability. Since liaisons may be the first point of contact with social cataloging sites when selecting books for purchase (single unit purchases), these librarians could share data that should be linked. This bibliographic information could make a difference in the discoverability of books in Indigenous languages.

The Print and Digital Presence

In 2011, Amazon announced that they were selling more Kindle ebooks than print paperbacks ("Amazon reported"). Somehow, this announcement must have felt like a premonition of the disappearance of the print book. Then, in 2020, the digital book industry for academic monographs gained notoriety when access to physical materials was limited in academic libraries during the COVID-19 pandemic. During this time, everyday conversations about favoring ebooks over print books in academic acquisitions kindled our reflection on the print and ebook presence and their significance for Indigenous publications. One notion is noticeable: while digitizing Indigenous books is vital for access in emergency lockdowns, maintaining the print book market is needed to balance the representation of Indigenous works in canon-heavy built academic collections.

Comparison studies between ebooks and print books concerning circulation, user perception, convenience, reading experience, and format preference have been relevant since the 2000s with mixed results. For example, some studies have compared these two formats to identical titles. Cathy Goodwin examined print and ebook use for identical titles in the e-Duke Scholarly Collection. She found that print books were used more in particular areas (history and social sciences), while ebooks matched print book usage in music, art, and literature (101–105). The usefulness of providing both formats for identical titles was one of the concluding points three researchers from the University of Toronto Libraries found when they analyzed format preferences by constituents from this university for three academic book publishers. One of the findings showed that when comparing title usage by format (print-only, online-only, and both formats), patrons used both formats (print and ebook) more than the online-only or print-only formats, with a slight preference for print books overall (Yuan et al. 36).

Although the University of Toronto is only one study, this finding invites us to examine whether purchasing both formats for an identical title makes sense in times of evolving technology and issues with budgets and storage space (Yuan et al. 29). In an ideal setting, publishers and book vendors would maintain the supply of a title continuously. While this idyllic environment may be a reality for those few mass-appeal books, the Indigenous literature market is much smaller. These books tend to be published in print format, in small quantities, and with a prognosis placing these books at high risk of being out of publication. To illustrate, the second edition of the short stories book *Choconoy* by Mayan Mam author Wilson Fernando Loayes Orozco has been published as a limited edition of 50 copies only. Similarly, the title *La sombra del perro*, a short story book by Mayan Mam author Tulio López, is also available in a limited edition of 50 copies.[7] These two books exemplify not only the time frailness of Indigenous publication but also the small quantity available in the market.

From the point of view of the librarian with collection development responsibility, while relying only on ebooks is appropriate for some areas of knowledge, print purchasing appears sensible for books of literary esteem that represent the creative literary work of underrepresented writers, such as Indigenous authors. Thus, when funding allows, purchasing print books and their electronic counterpart makes sense to provide access, especially where natural disasters and health-driven closures are a real possibility in higher education.

As mentioned before, access is critical when considering the acquisition of identical titles in print and electronic format. The premise is that hybrid collection and development of Indigenous literature will enhance teaching and learning by facilitating faculty and student access to these materials. Indigenous authors from Latin America appear to recognize the need for access and distribution of their work in the first quarter of the 21st century as several authors have used open-access Internet sites, such as *Musuq Illa-Harawikuna Runasimipi, Gusanos de la Memoria*, and *Círculo de Poesía*, to publish poems and short stories. Internet sites promoting Indigenous literature in an open-access digital environment could complement academic collections with linked data to read alike or more works by an author, particularly when Indigenous authors publish their works as solo pieces and not as part of a book.

We have argued that the "metaphor of the window" for acquisition practices of Indigenous books offers a broader approach to collection development open to non-canonical works, transforming the repository notion of an academic library into a constantly evolving one. Building a collection of Indigenous literature presents remarkable opportunities for teaching and learning, the development of cultural consciousness connected to Indigenous knowledge, and societal changes toward Indigenous people. However, this collection will also challenge librarians and users with discoverability for which BIBED could provide a workable path to connect students and faculty to Indigenous literature. Finally, as access to Indigenous literary works will be contingent on hybrid purchase practices considering print and ebooks, sustaining print acquisition of these books could guarantee an avenue to balance the representation of different types of knowledge in academic collections.

Notes

1 Language brokering is another area of study examining children who act as translators for their immigrant families, see Alejandro Morales and William E. Hanson, "Language Brokering: An Interactive Review of the Literature."

2 Interdisciplinary scholars investigating language brokering on youth who translate for their immigrant family members noted the importance of transcultural skills, seen as understanding different cultural perspectives, a crucial competence in a globalized world; see Guan et al., "Translating into Understanding," 335.
3 The concept of hegemony in libraries has been discussed in their role in maintaining dominance by certain societal groups.
4 Carol Benson suggests that a multilingual habitus in education benefits all learners; see Chapter 15, *Language Issues in Comparative Education*. Terry Lamb suggests a shift from a monolingual to a plurilingual habitus in the urban school; see "Towards a Plurilingual Habitus."
5 Referring to ethics in cataloging by exploring the "right way" to meet users' needs, Gretchen L. Hoffman argues that users should be defined not as individuals but as a group of people or domains (nurses or college students), and standards should mirror these users' needs.
6 Hobart clarifies that later on, authority records were added for "Musqueam First Nation" and "Musqueam dialect" (61).
7 Libros Centroamericanos. "RE: Guatemalan Literature by Mayan Authors Oct. 2023." Received by Kathia Ibacache, 11 October 2023.

3 How to Decolonize and Indigenize the Curriculum

Javier Muñoz-Díaz and Leila Gómez

This chapter discusses principles and strategies to engage with Indigenous Latin American and Latinx materials in U.S. higher education curricula, including language teaching, area studies, ethnic studies, and beyond the hegemonic disciplinaries boundaries between humanities, social sciences, and natural sciences. As stated in the introduction, our proposal for collaboration between librarians and faculty aims to facilitate access to materials *by or with* Indigenous peoples rather than *about* Indigenous peoples. The outcomes of this collaboration are non-hegemonic library collections and course curricula that serve all students by showcasing heterogeneous and underrepresented backgrounds, including the diverse amalgamations of indigeneity with race, class, gender, sexual orientation, and disability throughout the Americas. In the specific case of inclusive curriculum, we follow the principles outlined by Jairo I. Fúnez-Flores:

> The coloniality of curriculum is understood as an imperial/colonial doctrine insofar as it is conceived as a pedagogical mode of imperial domination aimed at colonial domesticity and capitalist exploitation. This conceptualization seeks to contribute to understanding the complex way the dominant curriculum propagates and articulates an imperial/colonial sense of being indifferent towards the suffering of the colonized and racialized others ... not only within a specific nation-state but also within a planetary frame. (14)

Fúnez-Flores builds upon Aníbal Quijanos's "coloniality of power," which describes the global pattern of domination that stems from a geopolitical division of labor between European/white and non-European/non-white subjects. Quijanos's and Fúnez-Florez's decolonial framework established a linkage between material/political-economic dispossession and discursive/symbolic erasure of Indigenous peoples and other marginalized populations. This pattern of domination showed that knowledge produced in the centers of imperial power (what is called the Western

DOI: 10.4324/9781032660561-4

world or the Global North) becomes the pennants of progress. In contrast, knowledge produced in the colonized regions (what is called the Global South) is stripped of relevancy or considered a mere input for the Global North's "centers of calculation" (Latour). This "geopolitics of curriculum" (Fúnez-Flores 16) reduces racialized subjects to mere informants (if not mere objects of study) rather than agents of knowledge production.

Decolonization is a radical project, but neoliberal multiculturalism and identity politics downplay it. In these instances, decolonization becomes a metaphor or a commodity rather than a radical praxis that engages with sites of struggle against systems of domination. When discussing the decolonization of the curriculum, we must move beyond the filling of representation quotas, such as having a few Indigenous texts to balance a cannon traditionally composed of several Eurocentric materials. Decolonization of the curriculum's aim is not limited to fixing or adjusting colonial distortions that ravage discursive/symbolic production *about* Indigenous peoples. According to John Guillory, the curriculum and educational institutions are not primarily concerned with reproducing cultural values (by selecting, interpreting, and teaching the most significant works that reveal the universal human spirit) but with reproducing social relations. By participating in academic institutions, Eurocentric subjects and racialized subjects do not find themselves on equal footing concerning knowledge: "The school does not exist merely to lift a veil of ignorance [...]. The school functions as a system of credentialization by which it produces a specific *relation* to culture. That relation is different from different people, which is to say that it reproduces social relations" (Guillory 56). In other words, the white ethno-class (Eurocentric subjectivities) becomes the universal subject of knowledge production, while racialized people are reduced to objects of inquiry.

To fulfill the decolonization of the curriculum's goal, we must highlight how academic institutions participate in the material dispossession of Indigenous people's livelihood at both local and global scale. For instance, it is imperative to recognize the colonial foundations of U.S. academic institutions that legitimized a Eurocentric subject position and developed technologies for controlling and managing racialized people. The current marketization of higher education in neoliberal times seems to be at odds with the traditional Western university and the liberal arts curriculum; however, the neoliberal restructuring of the university (austerity policies and job precarity) continues the politics of dispossession against racialized bodies that founded the Eurocentric academia in the first place (Stein 4). Non-hegemonic curricula should confront how discursive/symbolic and material dispossessions are intertwined.

The following section will explain how the decolonization of the curriculum could occur in different disciplines and fields related to Indigenous Latin American and Latinx peoples. We start with language departments (such as Spanish or Hispanic studies), which are the fields that traditionally have dealt with the cultural production of Latin America and its diaspora. Our major critique of these programs is Hispanismo ideology, the ingrained Eurocentrism that structures its scaffolding. Then, we move to interdisciplinary studies programs and departments, such as Latin American and Latinx studies. Although these programs strive to decenter assimilationist perspectives in higher education, they are still grounded in Eurocentrism as the material ground of the research and teaching. Finally, the chapter will review how to incorporate Indigenous epistemologies to challenge hegemonic understanding of science in the curriculum.

Against Hispanismo in Spanish-Language Programs

Based on a quantitative survey of over a hundred Spanish departments in U.S. higher education, Jeffrey Herlihy-Mera states that "US departments hire faculty in Spanish-language cultural fields through a framework that is overwhelmingly Eurocentric" (34). Although Spain only concentrates roughly 10% of the Spanish-speaking population worldwide, the data outline the overrepresentation of Spain in faculty research interest and course themes throughout the U.S. higher education system, leading to a ratio 1:1 between Peninsular and Latin American languages and literatures (35–36).[1] Herlihy-Mera's indictment focuses on doctoral-granting institutions since, following academia's hierarchical scaffolding, these institutions provide credentials to participate at lower levels of language and cultural studies instruction. In other words, perceived elite institutions' Eurocentric curricula establish social relations to knowledge production that are reproduced throughout the academic apparatus. These social relations elevate a Eurocentric subject position that, in the case of the Spanish language, erases Spanish-speaking communities in the United States, such as the Southwest region or Puerto Rico.

What Herlihy-Mera's research found is actually an open secret among faculty and graduate students in Spanish departments. Nobody was caught off guard when these data were released, but they still constitute a shocking corroboration of the rampant Eurocentrism in Spanish-language and cultural field programs. Although this survey is concerned with the overrepresentation of Spain to the detriment of U.S. Spanish-speaking communities, we believe it could also support a critique of the erasure of Indigenous Latin American and Latinx languages and cultures.

In 2012, when Javier Muñoz-Díaz started the Master of Arts program in Spanish at one of the top 25 perceived elite institutions, the faculty ratio

between Peninsular and Latin American scholars was roughly equal
(1:1). At the time, the MA program aimed to train generalist scholars
knowledgeable of the Spanish literary canon. Instead of writing and
defending a thesis, the MA student must pass a comprehensive exam based
on reading lists. In accordance with the faculty demographics, the reading
lists also had an equal ratio (1:1) between research areas in Peninsular
and Latin American cultures. Moving beyond Herlihy-Mera's critique,
the issue at hand was not only the underrepresentation of Latin
American literary production (a region that comprises three-quarters of
the Spanish-speaking people) but a misrepresentation that stems from a
Latin American canon that follows Eurocentric principles. Muñoz-Díaz
was assigned a traditional Latin American reading list epitomizing
the Criollo-mestizo elite. It only marginally includes materials about
Indigenous peoples (mostly from Mesoamerica and the Andes), while
materials in Indigenous languages were absent. A similar erasure occurred
with Afro-descendants and other global diasporas appearing sporadically
throughout the list. However, the most intriguing omission was materials
by Latinx people who use English as their literary language.

The low readership in Indigenous languages is a well-known excuse
for excluding these materials from Latin American reading lists.
However, what is the logic behind the exclusion of materials written in
English by the Latin American diaspora in North America? The
disavowal of literary texts written in a language other than Spanish
follows a colonizing and Eurocentric ideology called Hispanismo. This
ideology has been the cornerstone of Spanish-language instruction in
U.S. higher education due to the work of George Ticknor (1791–1871),
who imposed a philological model that subordinated culture instruction
to language proficiency. In other words, the study of a given culture (e.g.,
"Spanish," "French," or "German") relies on the teaching of its
language. The fact that the culture/language model has primarily served
to learn European imperial languages (leaving behind the languages
spoken in their former or current colonies) speaks about how this
academic model reproduces the coloniality of power.

Meanwhile, the Real Academia Española (founded in 1713), whose
emblem is "limpia, fija y da esplendor" ("cleans, fixes, and gives
splendor"), started opening chapters in Latin American countries in
the second half of the 19th century (the first one being the Academia
Colombiana de la Lengua, in 1871). At a time when Spain had lost its
political and economic control over its former colonies, its elites sought
to establish cultural dominance over territories that would become the
Spanish-speaking world. This neo-imperial project (embodied by other
state-sponsored institutions such as the Instituto Cervantes) is clearly
stated in the institution's mission: "ensure that the Spanish language, in
its continuous adaptation to the needs of its speakers, does not break its

essential unity" (Real Academia Española). To preserve such a precious linguistic unity, Latin American countries become neo-colonies in a cultural imperialist project. Hispanismo participates in the coloniality of power by disseminating a universalistic and philological approach to Spanish language diversity, stating that Latin American linguistic and cultural expressions should be understood as emanations from a common root located in the Iberian Peninsula. In other words, "the language in Spain remains the norm in relation to which all innovation and change are variations subject to scrutiny before inclusion" (Castro-Klaren 11). Supposedly, Hispanismo foregrounds a hemispheric and transcontinental commonality among the Spanish-speaking countries, promoting a horizontal exchange among cultural agents. In fact, a hierarchical setting posits European Spanish (in itself a fabrication that erases linguistic diversity in the Iberian peninsula) as the standard language while promoting "a false brotherhood that traffics in Latin American authors and texts from a perspective of tutelage" (Falconí Trávez 29). This colonizing dynamic also influences the teaching of heritage Spanish speakers in the United States, who are expected to join Spanish departments "to learn how to read literary text, and thus experience a reinforcement of the 'correct' and literary uses of the language" (Castro-Klaren 8). This is the logic behind the exclusion of Chicanx and Latinx cultural productions written in English—such texts and materials are regarded as foreign to the mission of Spanish departments, which is to teach the standardized version of the language.

Castro-Klarén provocatively suggests that the Spanish major should include English courses to disrupt the language-culture dyad entrenched by the philological foundations of U.S. language departments. The rationale for English courses includes better serving students whose first language is not Spanish (6) and engaging with scholarly production written in English, particularly about Indigenous texts such as the *Popol Vuh* (14). The irony is that Castro-Klarén's provocation is currently a harsh reality. Given the decrease in enrollment numbers in humanities, some small language departments have relied on offering English courses focused on cultural studies to survive budget cuts in the neoliberal university.

Although some Spanish faculty members (e.g., those affiliated with Hispanismo) may see the inclusion of English courses as treason to the language department's mission, other faculty may appreciate the opening of these courses as an opportunity to include materials that would not appropriately fit in a traditional upper-division course of the Spanish major. Muñoz-Díaz's course "Indigenous Peoples in Latin America" is an example of an English course incorporating multilingual materials produced by Indigenous peoples and spoken/written in Indigenous languages. This course's inception derives from the current Indigenous language's reclamation movement, expressed in the growing production of films and digital media in Indigenous languages from the Americas. Muñoz-Díaz also incorporates these multilingual materials in upper-division courses conducted in Spanish, but their assignments are ultimately subordinate to developing students' Spanish proficiency. Therefore, such a course stands in a balance between second-language acquisition and cultural studies fields, an approach known as content-based language instruction. Unfortunately, given the traditional Spanish curriculum's scaffolding in which such a course is located, Indigenous materials are subordinated to Hispanismo ideologies that regard Indigeneity not as a legitimate matter of inquiry (that would be the subject of disciplines such as anthropology or linguistics), but as a particularity subordinated to the study of Spanish language in the former colonies.

In an ideal situation, the class discussion of an Indigenous film should take place in the languages used in the film. However, we propose that, instead of subordinating the teaching of Indigenous films to developing language proficiency, such courses should highlight the power dynamics between the languages spoken in the materials. Film and digital media *by/with* Indigenous peoples tend to be multilingual works, including sections in colonial languages that offer opportunities to discuss power dynamics in the context of internal colonization. Films such as *Retablo* or *Ixcanul* contain significant sections spoken in Spanish that laid out colonizing dynamics regarding Indigenous peoples' land, bodies, and identities.[2] However, the analysis of power dynamics between Spanish and Quechua or Maya-Kaqchikel should not be limited to developing proficiency in a target language (including standard and academic English). An equally productive engagement with these issues will happen if students employ their first language in class discussion, whether it be Spanish, English, Quechua, or Maya-Kaqchikel.

Although Hispanismo was challenged by the development of Latinoamericanismo and the influence of ethnic studies from the 1970s, it remains a leverage force in scaffolding the curricula in Latin American cultural studies.[3] A contestation of this colonizing Eurocentric perspective requires an active engagement with materials produced by minoritized and underrepresented peoples, such as Latin American and Latinx Indigenous peoples, and might include requiring master's and doctoral students to learn an Indigenous language before earning their degree (Gómez 5). Indigenous language instruction should not be limited to graduate students specializing in Indigenous cultures. Instead, universities' language departments should offer instruction in the Indigenous languages spoken in the territories where the institution is located. We understand that implementing an Indigenous language requirement seems like a time-consuming utopia devoid of institutional support (if not victim of immediate backlash). However, we believe that an active collaboration between librarians and faculty could facilitate the engagement with materials and resources indispensable for building such a decolonial curriculum.

Against Mestizaje and Indigenismo in Latin American and Latinx Studies

As we mentioned in the previous section, Indigenous languages and cultures only appear marginally in Spanish teaching programs because, per Hispanismo, they privilege political affiliations to Latin American nation-states that impose Spanish as their official language. Interestingly, a similar exclusion occurs in Latin American study programs that deterritorialize indigeneity following the logic of U.S.-based area studies and mestizaje/indigenista nationalist discourses from Latin America. In other words, the Indigenous identity marker of Latin American and Latinx people is replaced by a national one (Peruvian, Argentinian, Chilean, etc.). To properly showcase indigeneity in Latin American and Latinx studies, it is necessary to strengthen the connections of this interdisciplinary field with Latinoamericanismo and ethnic studies rather than with area studies. On the other hand, we also propose to embrace the proposal of Critical Latinx Indigeneities (Blackwell, Boj Lopez, and Urrieta Jr), a critical intervention that compound the fields of Native American and Indigenous studies, Latinx studies, and Latin American studies. Particularly, Critical Latinx Indigeneities will allow us to counteract the white-criollo perspective still founded in Latinoamericanismo's canon.

The inception of area studies dates to the aftermath of World War II and the intricacies of Cold War politics. The United States's national security needs require producing academic knowledge about compartmentalized world geographies. The irony is that "the United States and Europe are not areas of studies for Third World countries. On the contrary, Europe and the United States provide 'models' to study the Third World" (Mignolo 36). In other words, the model of area studies is an iteration of the geopolitics of knowledge that, using the methodological frame of the social sciences, reduced Latin America to an object of study and Latin American intellectuals to informers. On the other hand, we found Latinoamericanismo or Pensamiento Crítico in Latin America, which is opposite to area studies on the colonial divide. That is to say, Latin America reclaims its status as knowledge producer about socio-economic dynamics that impact the periphery of global capitalism. Moreover, while knowledge production by area studies scholars is supposedly "objective," Latinoamericanismo assumes a "personal and political involvement" that, interestingly, is also found in U.S.-based Latinx studies due to the framework provided by ethnic studies (Mignolo 65). The Cold War also witnessed the formation of ethnic studies fields due to social movements that denounced the limitation of U.S. liberalism and criticized internal colonialism in the country. According to Juan Poblete, ethnic studies articulates a U.S. sociopolitical shift in which the "figure of the 'immigrant assimilating' was displaced by the insurgent colonized in a struggle against cultural, political, racial, and economic domination" (xi). While area studies focus on the compartmentalized world geography subjected to global power's influences, ethnic studies engage with colonizing dynamics that affect global diasporas (racialized people by the coloniality of power) within the U.S. territory. Pedro Cabán succinctly outlines the difference between these fields of study: "Latin American Studies was a top-down enterprise promoted by government agencies, university administrators, and large foundations. In contrast, ethnic studies programs were interested in studying the 'Third World within' the United States, and linking these studies to the 'Third World'" (222). Although ethnic studies are currently institutionalized and might sever the needs of state-sponsored multiculturalism (Mignolo 56), the paradigm shift that it prompted in U.S. higher education would elicit a new configuration of Latin American studies. Its current rebranding as Latin American and Latinx studies is a positive move, but it should recognize that the placement of Indigenous materials is still marginal in this new configuration.

The reason for the ongoing marginalization of indigeneity in Latin America and Latinx studies is the persistence of mestizaje and indigenismo ideologies. Both are liberal discourses that, nevertheless, reproduce the coloniality of power. In Latin American countries, *Mestizaje* is the celebration of racial miscegenation and cultural hybridization that, nevertheless, promotes racial whitening. On the other hand, indigenismo is the celebration of Indigenous monumental heritage that, at the same time, demands the modernization/acculturation of Indigenous peoples. To challenge the gravitation of these ideologies in Latin America and Latinx studies, we promote Critical Latinx Indigeneities. This emerging interdisciplinary field discusses the migration of Indigenous Latin American peoples to North America, which means that Indigenous people become settlers in the homeland of other U.S. Native American people while still facing marginalization from colonizing institutions and hybrid hegemonies (Blackwell, Boj Lopez, and Urrieta Jr 127–8). This critical intervention discusses how the Latinx, Chicanx, or Hispanic identity markers erases indigeneity while also promoting

> the acknowledgement and consideration of the complex, multilayered, and multi-vocal ways of being Indigenous, especially those being

recognized, developed, deployed, and negotiated across national (colonial and Indigenous) borders through overlapping colonialities and settler states and within migrant transregions, which often cross multiple ethnoracial structures. (129–130)

Critical Latinx Indigeneities allow us to overcome the limitations of Latinoamericanismo, which was traditionally enacted by the white-criollo elite from Latin America and still reproduces mestizaje ideologies that subordinate, appropriate, and erase Indigeneity. On the other hand, classical Chicanx and Latinx scholarship was influenced by Mexican state-sponsored-indigenismo, which celebrates Aztec imperial mythologies but dilutes the role of Indigenous peoples throughout the Mexico-U.S. border (Saldaña-Portillo).

As an example of the necessity to center the migration of Indigenous Latin American people and life experiences of Indigenous Latinx people, we will discuss Peruvian anthropologist Marisol de la Cadena's testimony, which is a common experience for other Latin American immigrants of white-Criollo and mestizo upbringing (including the authors of this chapter):

> In 1994—shortly after I had migrated from Peru to the United States—I met a man in Santa Fe, New Mexico. He was an artist, wore his hair long in a ponytail, and spoke what struck me as "fluid English." Trained in the Peruvian cultural perception of race (which I had not yet revisited) I had no doubt that the man was "mestizo." Weeks later I learned I was mistaken: "I am a Native American," he told me, and added: "Aren't you a Peruvian Indian too?" I answered that I was not–and my explanation confused him. Although my skin is brown, and I have "Indian looking" features, in Peru most people consider me white. Perhaps some would accept it if I selfidentify as "mestiza," but everybody would laugh at me if I claimed to be "Indian." (261)

This anecdote not only illustrates the sociocultural nature of all racial distinctions (there is nothing "natural" or "biological" in race), but also highlights the challenges of negotiating Latin American mestizo identities within North American ethnoracial structures. First, we need to acknowledge that people of Latin American origin are racialized in the United States, but these people also have internal racial/class divisions that might pass unnoticed in the Global North (e.g., Afro-Latinx or Indigenous Latinx). Second, these same ethnoracial structures are diluted by the Latin American diaspora (including Latinoamericanismo in the diaspora), who still carried the impact of state-sponsored mestizaje and indigenismo ideologies.

How to Decolonize and Indigenize the Curriculum   57

Mestizaje and indigenismo ideologies started as nationalistic projects by Latin American white-criollo elites to consolidate their political rule while navigating the impact of U.S. imperialism. For this reason, both ideologies are rooted in the (supposedly) stark differences between the British colonization in North America and the Spanish/Portuguese colonization in Latin America, a binary that explains the socioeconomic character of each subcontinental region and its specific relation to Indigenous peoples. On one hand, the term "settler colonialism" is widely used in the English-speaking world to describe "a form of imperialism wherein colonizers occupy and remain on stolen colonized land, recreating the social structures, economic systems and political power within that region … . [Settler colonialism] comes with the erasure of indigenous peoples' ways of knowing, being, and living" (Jaffee and Casey 624). There are also two forms of settler colonialism: 1) external/extractive, when the metropole does not settle permanently in the colonies, and 2) internal, when the colonizers remain in a stolen territory and reproduce social dynamics that benefit them as an elite (625). On the other hand, settler colonialism is a precise descriptor of British imperialism's legacies, but it has some points of contact as well as limitations when applied to the waves of colonization in Latin America. One of these main differences is related to the processes and politics of racial miscegenation and cultural hybridization in Latin American countries. To address these particularities, indigenismo, mestizaje and their aftermaths were highly theorized in Latin America by intellectuals, artists, and scientists, while politicians and policymakers used them as key concepts.

De la Cadena explains the double-hybridity of the term "mestizo" in Peru and other Latin American countries due to the juxtaposition of two Western "regimes of knowledge": "Holy fait (later known as religion) and scientific reason" (262). While Anglo-Saxon America primarily follows the later regime and understands the mestizo as the miscegenation of two discrete races, Latin America combines both regimes (religion and science) and regards the mestizo as a racially and culturally defined body at the same time (269). For this reason, someone with Indigenous heritage would become mestizo (less native and more white-criollo) if they are assimilated into Eurocentric institutions such as the church and the school. On the other hand, the imposed flexibility of Indigenous race/culture would allow Latin American nation-states to promote a mestizo national identity—that is to say, an identity shared by the whole population that is also (a little, just enough) Indigenous. Chapter 1 discussed the ambiguity of racial/ethnic affiliation in Latin America using the examples of two canonical Peruvian writers: César Vallejo, one mestizo with Indigenous physical traits who didn't speak an Indigenous language, and José María Arguedas, another mestizo without Indigenous phenotype but fully immersed in Indigenous languages since his childhood. However, we can ignore the fact that both canonical writers, although mestizos in the Peruvian context and racialized when traveling to the Global North, participated in and benefited from Latin American white-criollo institutions (including critical and decolonial brands such as Latinoamericanismo). People of similar backgrounds and personal journeys than Vallejo's and Arguedas's have the right to explore and articulate their relationship to indigeneity (this includes the authors of this chapter), but without ignoring the actual stark differences between Latin American elite migration experience and Indigenous Latin American migrants who are disenfranchised from both Latin American and U.S. nation-states, as well as Latinx communities. The ongoing migration crisis at the Mexico-U.S. border and the Guatemala-Mexico border (in which a significant number of migrants are Indigenous people) demand us to be critical of the racial/class division that mestizaje and indigenismo still face.

Indigenous Materials Beyond Area Studies and Ethnic Studies

In prompting an engagement with materials *by/with* Indigenous Latin American and Latinx peoples, our aim is not limited to the curriculum of a single academic discipline, but it aspires to be transversal to the whole higher education scaffolding. For that reason, after analyzing the placement of indigeneity in Latin American and Latinx studies, we now move to discuss how to employ Indigenous knowledge/praxis to challenge the hegemonic epistemological boundaries among culture, politics, and science.

To engage with Indigenous materials beyond hegemonic disciplinary compartmentation, we follow Wesley Leonard's proposal of "language reclamation" as part of a larger decolonization struggle rooted in Indigenous epistemologies (19). While the "language revitalization" model usually focuses on increasing the number of speakers with grammatical proficiency, the "language reclamation" model serves Indigenous communities' needs by showcasing their understanding of what "language" and "culture" means. Thus, this model implies challenging the disciplinary boundaries of linguistics or anthropology (in which the study of Indigenous materials is traditionally confined) as well as the protocols of scientific research and academic writing. For instance, by limiting Quechua's understanding of "nature" to the discipline of anthropology, it becomes a matter of "cultural difference" or "cultural diversity" that is still subordinated to Eurocentric epistemologies of what knowledge is and how it is acquired. Instead, we propose to place Indigenous understandings of topics such as "nature" and "body" at the center of other disciplines, including the fields of science, technology, engineering, and mathematics (STEM).

In *Braiding Sweetgrass*, Robin Wall Kimmerer, a scientist and member of the Potawatomi nation, provides another example of how to challenge Eurocentric scientific knowledge with Indigenous epistemologies. This author explains that "there is a barrier of language and meaning between science and traditional knowledge, different ways of knowing, different ways of communicating" (158). In the technical writing of academia, there needs to be an introduction, a literature review, a hypothesis, methods, results, discussion, conclusion, acknowledgment, and references cited—not to mention that the whole process needs to be approved by authoritative figures in the discipline, be they professors in a dissertation committee, or referees in a journal, or external reviewers.

In the chapter "Mishkos Kenomagwen: the Teaching of Grass," Kimmerer describes how Indigenous knowledge and practice follow an alternative path that nonetheless contributes greatly to our understanding of nature, even in ways that contradict science. She narrates the story of one of her students who, at the request of basket makers, wanted to see if different ways of harvesting might be the cause of sweetgrass disappearance. This student's literary review was not only that of the scientific scholarship but mainly listening to the elders and learning from them about the positive impact of sweetgrass harvesting. The student's methodology, which consisted of reproducing harvesting according to Indigenous practice, despite being questioned and devalued by her dissertation committee's professors, proved that "harvesting thinned the population, allowing the remaining shoots to respond to the extra space and light by reproducing quickly ... when it's gently tugged, the stem breaks and all those buds produce thrifty young shoots to fill the gap" (164). This story tells how difficult it is to get scientists to consider the validity of Indigenous knowledge in academia—it is, according to Wall Kimmerer, "like swimming upstream in cold, cold water" (160).

As we mentioned in the introduction, pluriversal knowledge (a world of many worlds) facilitates the recognition of Indigenous epistemologies beyond the logic of multiculturalism and identity politics. In the context of the Anthropocene (and the impending planetary destruction due to the capitalist mode of production), Mario Blaser and Marisol de la Cadena ask for participating in the divergence of global epistemologies (Indigenous and other marginalized ones) by means of confronting the incommensurability and excess that characterized cross-cultural exchange. For instance, Guaraní Indigenous peoples consider that forest animals are also sacred entities that have a legitimate seat in political disputes (2). Western epistemology (the "one-world" of multiculturalism) regards such a belief as an example of "animism," a characteristic of pre-modern or non-Eurocentric cultures that lacks an understanding of science and what the natural world is. However, we should be willing to "reckon with the idea that much of what the discipline deemed cultural beliefs might be *not only* such" (Blaser and De la Cadena 17). Maybe the current global climate crisis could be better managed if we engage with Indigenous understanding of nature beyond the logic of global capitalism.

Conclusion

There is still active resistance among scholars (e.g., language instructors and literary critics) toward decolonization of the curriculum. As Ramos and Daly explain:

> Because decoloniality critiques Europe, and because Europe has been seen as the geopolitical site from which writing, thinking, disciplines, and languages have been imposed onto its former colonies, literature scholars seem to be, at times, particularly resistant to decolonial theory, which calls into question the very foundations of our training, practices, and intellectual work. (Ramos and Daly, xxi)

We must state that decolonial critique is not a clear-cut and straightforward process. It is not the return to some sort of Indigenous purity that remains unfettered from the corruptions of coloniality/modernity. Students should not engage with Indigenous languages and cultures using a romanticized gaze that regards them as a new iteration of the bon savage. Decolonial critique implies recognizing how the global pattern of power (based on the geographical distribution of race, labor, and knowledge) manifests in each specific historical and sociocultural circumstance. The study of a given Indigenous language should embrace the "impurity" that characterizes sociocultural exchanges, including the impact of the colonial languages and cultures. According to Ramos and Daly, "fully rejecting [...] informed and cultural analysis of languages, literatures, and cultures simply because they are Eurocentric in origin all too readily plays into the logic of exclusion enacted through the diverse modalities of coloniality/modernity that Europe envisioned and instituted" (xvii). The creation of Indigenous language requirements and programs implies understanding Indigenous cultures as one of many participants in networks of exchange, patterns of domination, and movements of resistance.

Notes

1 According to Herlihy-Mera's findings, in the case of the top 25 perceived elite institutions, Peninsular language and cultural studies represent 47% of faculty research interest. A similar inflation occurs in the top 10 largest U.S. universities by enrollment (46% of faculty research on Spain), flagship

institutions in the southern border states (39%), and schools of 5,000+ students with over 50% Latinx enrollment (37%).
2 For a detailed analysis of both films and assignments that address the coloniality of power and gender, see Chapter 4.
3 Although Sara Castro-Klarén offers an insightful analysis of what we call (following Fúnez-Flores) the "coloniality of the curriculum," her examples of decolonial gestures in Spanish departments still follow the 1–1 ratio between Europe and the Americas, such as the courses "Comparative Historical Avant Gardes in Iberia and Latin America" and "Surrealism in Latin America and Spain" (10).

4 The Power of Healing and Indigenizing Feminism in the Classroom

Leila Gómez and Javier Muñoz-Díaz

We are aware that a policy of mere inclusion of Indigenous language instruction in higher education is not enough to achieve the goal of deep healing. Therefore, it has been important from the beginning to be clear about our values and objectives in creating a new curriculum. We were not looking for just a cosmetic reform or a simple fix of the education system to make it less oppressive or racist. Instead, we hope to work holistically, encompassing broader contexts along with the teaching of Indigenous languages and cultures, creating frameworks that generate spaces for deep healing, and transforming the roots of systemic and historical damage. At the same time, we seek to denounce other frameworks, such as the mere inclusion of diversity, that have sabotaged decolonizing efforts by reinforcing colonial power without transforming hegemonic power structures (McCaslin and Breton 4). Sisseton Wahpeton Oyate Professor at the University of Alberta, Kim TallBear, has discussed how DEI politics often include Indigenous and other marginalized groups, yet force them to adapt to institutional norms as opposed to undertaking institutional change (TallBear, "Beyond Diversity & Inclusion").

In an Indigenous healing framework, it is necessary to incorporate not only Indigenous languages but also what they bring with them: ancestral knowledge, practices, and traditions. In this new framework, spaces of harmony and balance can be generated within the community, with the bodies, the territories, and their spiritual dimensions: "Indigenous knowledge is based on a profound and thorough awareness of our relatedness in all directions: […] in this context, healing [is] not about 'fixing' individuals but about transforming relationships. It was always about 'being good relatives' to each other" (McCaslin and Breton 9). Outlining the process of healing as a four-season (winter, spring, summer, and fall) cycle, "colonialism" is the main challenge:

> The challenge of the fourth stage is to address the deeper structures that give rise to harm, so that healing and transformation can

continue down to the roots of what is causing imbalance and disharmony. Colonialism cannot continue unnamed, as if it were an invisible backdrop or neutral bystander to harm. It must be brought front and center and named as the root cause. Healing without this level of decolonizing transformation may temporarily fix immediate breakdowns, but it will not address the structures that led to them. Similar harms will recur. (McCaslin and Breton 12)

In this healing process, colonialism must not remain unnamed, and neither can Western scientific thought, prejudices, expectations, and behaviors legitimized by Global North institutions of knowledge to the detriment of Indigenous knowledge. The dynamics of oppression must be called as such and thus be made visible in our classes and libraries, because these dynamics of oppression are what have for centuries prevented Indigenous people from having access not only to education but also to housing, health, banks, jobs, etc. Such colonial dynamics have generated land dispossession, erasure of cultures and languages, assimilation, diaspora, genocides, and intergenerational trauma. A profound transformative and regenerative force cannot exclude the complex reality of colonial damage. The first step is acknowledging that colonialism is the root of harm.

In this more comprehensive framework, geopolitical questions arise that address the academic dynamics of the Global North and the Global South, particularly regarding the meaning of teaching Latin American Indigenous languages and cultures in the North American academy, which itself is based on territories expropriated from Native Americans. The teaching of these languages and cultures raises questions about external colonialism, internal colonialism, and settler colonialism, which cannot be answered separately. In Gómez's classes, particularly in the Department of Women and Gender Studies, the Indigenous "feminisms" of Abiayala have suggested ways to articulate all these questions around the territorial problem. The colonialism of power, gender, languages, knowledge, displacements, and migrations, the fight for environmental justice, green colonialism, and so many other modes of colonialism intersect and connect with the territorial problem: the land problem.

Is it possible to examine Indigenous feminism in the Global South in the same terms we use to discuss it in the Global North? A single definition of Indigenous feminism is problematic because Indigenous women's circumstances vary both in colonial societies (where patriarchy dominates) and in Indigenous communities (which have distinct histories and cultural traditions). However, although Indigenous women do not share a single culture, they do have a common colonial history. Through analysis of literature and films by Indigenous and non-Indigenous writers and filmmakers, Gómez's classes explore gender issues in Indigenous communities in the Americas that are tied to colonialism and land struggle. Indigenous feminisms share strategic alliances of solidarity with other transnational feminisms in the Global North and the Global South. Although these alliances may seem only temporary, they are urgent. As Linda Tuhiwai Smith reminds us, in the 21st century "a new agenda for indigenous activity [extends] ... beyond the decolonization aspirations of a particular indigenous community [and moves] ... towards the development of global 'indigenous strategic alliances'" (qtn. in Keme 47). On that note, Emil' Keme proposed a hemispheric "Abiayala" as a locus of enunciation and reclamation. From there, it is possible to imagine or re-imagine a world from the plurality of Indigenous experiences:

> Its epistemological articulation emerges against ideas of (Latin) America in order to counteract their colonial legacies and recover the hemisphere for Indigenous peoples. Abiayala offers us the possibility to articulate a collective locus of enunciation that goes beyond the borders imposed on us by Europeans and their descendants, the possibility to rethink and recover the world from our own epistemological millenarian legacies. (49)

Indigeneizing Feminism

Gómez's classes pose the challenge of teaching gender and indigeneity from a transnational perspective, where specific problems for women from different Indigenous nations of Turtle Island and Abiayala are studied. These problems revolve around three—inseparable—axes of coloniality: the coloniality of the land, linguistic coloniality, and the coloniality of gender. In this section, we will focus on Gómez's class titled "Gender and Indigeneity in Film and Literature of the Americas." As the title suggests, the course incorporates literary texts and films by Indigenous and non-Indigenous authors and directors in different Indigenous languages of the Americas, including Quechua, Maya Kaqchikel, Mapudungun, and Lakota. Delete as Emil' Keme reminds us: "while it is important to celebrate [...] steps toward the creation of transhemispheric Indigenous bridges, we must not forget the fact that more than a thousand Indigenous languages survive in our hemisphere and that it is essential to generate support for the survival and revitalization of these languages. This must be one of our priorities" (48).

As indicated in the introduction, Gómez starts from the initial assumption that the dispossession of land is the first and permanent wound that runs through the experiences of Indigenous women of different origins and that this dispossession disrupts not only Indigenous gender structures but also languages and epistemes. This class also aims to challenge Western feminism as a field of study from the critical perspective of Indigenous women, for whom feminism is a form of imperialism of the Global North and the colonialism of white (criollo) and mestizo elites in the Global South; students, therefore, are expected to challenge their assumptions based on these dissonances.

Teaching a class on Indigenous women and gender in Abiayala at a university in the United States cannot be done without establishing correspondence with local settler colonialism. As Eve Tuck and Kwayne Yang have pointed out, in their essay "Decolonization Is Not a Metaphor," external colonialism cannot be separated from internal colonialism. At the same time, it cannot be ignored that our pedagogical practice may serve to reproduce practices of settler colonialism, even if it is based on principles of social and anti-colonial justice. To explore the connection between external and internal colonialism and settler colonialism, Gómez proposes for class discussion a corpus of non-fiction texts and films focused on the relationship with the land of Indigenous women from the north and south of the Americas.

The first of these films is *Daughter of the Lake* (2015), directed by Ernesto Cabellos. Set in the Andes, the plot follows the story of women who maintain different relationships with the land, lagoons, and minerals in Peru and Bolivia. On the one hand, a group of Indigenous women in Bolivia explains how the need to support their families forced them to work in the mines. On the other hand, a European woman tells how she redirected her jewelry business after traveling and learning about the harmful impact of gold extraction on the region. The story's protagonist, however, is Nélida, a law student and leader of popular and Indigenous movements against the Conga mining company. Due to her knowledge of the laws, her activism also consists of advising farmers on their rights to land ownership, rights that the government and the mining company want to usurp. Nélida is an Indigenous woman, and as such, she experiences considerable tension in moving between the countryside, the city, her life on the farm, and her studies in the city. The film beautifully narrates her communication with Mama Qocha (the lagoon) and her spirits, as well as the fear for her own life and the lives of those who work for environmental justice and the defense of the earth.

Daughter of the Lake begins the conversation that will continue throughout the course about Good Living (Sumaq Kawsay) and female leadership in movements for environmental justice. This conversation also addresses the fight for land and claims against violent dispossession and constant aggression that peasants suffer from the usurpation of the state and private companies that seek to take over the natural resources of the lands on which the peasants live. Nélida's case is similar to many well-known activists, such as Berta Isabel Cáceres Flores (1971–2016), a Lenca Indigenous leader and environmental activist in Honduras. Berta

Cáceres was assassinated for organizing, in collaboration with other people, "a grassroots campaign that successfully pressured the world's largest dam builder to pull out of the Agua Zarca Dam" at the Río Gualcarque. Berta Cáceres's murder was followed by those of two more activists and land defenders within the same month (Lakhani).

Because the land problem occupies a central place in the film's discussion, crucial Latin American texts are discussed, such as the seminal essay "The Land Problem" by José Carlos Mariátegui (1926) and texts on the agrarian reform carried out by President Juan Velasco Alvarado in the first decades of the second half of the 20th century in Peru. These provide a basic historical overview of the problem of land as a problem not only of a cultural or moral nature but also—significantly—of an economic and political nature. Understanding the history of the establishment and the dismantling of semi-feudal serfdom and *latifundio* is the main objective of this conversation with the students. Mariátegui's essay, "The Land Problem," serves as a good point of entrance to the land discussion since it clearly defines the root of the territorial issue in the Andes, from the colonial period to the independent republic. After the Independence from Spain, the landholding aristocracy (*criollos*, the elite European descendants) maintained its position of power as the dominant class in Peru, and there was no abolition of the Indigenous forced labor. Therefore, latifundism and feudalism remained intact and the republic inherited the colonial privileges. The peasant population, which in Peru was Indigenous, did not benefit directly or actively from the war of independence, and the revolutionary program did not represent its claims. Mariategui's proposal is at the center of Anibal Quijano's "Coloniality of Power," a text that is also discussed on several occasions later in the class. In *Daughter of the Lake*, this situation persists, despite the 1960s Agrarian Reform in Peru. The lot of land given to Máxima Acuña is under the threat of a mining company that is in alliance with the state and the military. The Conga Mining Company seeks to seize the land and the lagoon and remove Indigenous peoples from their territories.

Nélida's spiritual relationship with the lagoon is studied as a part of the Indigenous ancestral relationship with Pachamama. This spiritual relationship, which maintains the community link with the practices and knowledge of ancestral medicine and food sovereignty, expands in the discussion of other films in the course about the shamanism of Indigenous women, such as *Mama Irene, Healer of the Andes* (2022), directed by Bettina Ehrhardt and Elisabeth Mohlmann, and *Mothers of the Land* (2020), directed by Diego and Álvaro Sarmiento. Sumaq Kawsay is introduced here as a philosophy of Good Living, which is explained as a proposal against the industrialism of the Anthropocene in both capitalist and socialist economies. Sumaq Kawsay is living in

The Power of Healing and Indigenizing Feminism in the Classroom 67

harmony with people and with nature. It is the basis of the defense of nature, of life itself and of all humans and other-than-humans.

These movies are shown not only to students in class but also to the community with permission from the film directors. In that way, we seek to amplify the outreach and the conversation about Indigenous worldviews. *Mama Irene* and *Mothers of the Land* were part of the Quechua Film Series organized by the Latin American and Latinx Studies Center at CU Boulder in the fall semester of 2023. *Mama Irene*'s director, Elisabeth Möhlmann, and Magaly Quispe, the protagonist's niece, joined the conversation with students and other audience members after the screening. Claudia Arteaga and Odi Gonzales, both specialists in Quechua films and language, respectively, were part of the roundtable organized after the screening of *Mothers of the Land*.

Mama Irene portrays the life of a woman healer in the Sinakara Valley in the Andes, her healing methods, wisdom, and spiritual guidance for her community, particularly women and children. It is a story about Indigenous women's empowerment. The students in Gómez's class are asked to read and discuss a bibliography on the topic of Indigenous women healers, among which is Jessica Martínez-Cruz's chapter "This Knowledge Counts! Harmony and Spirituality in Miskitu Critical Thought". The chapter describes the successful way in which a well-known healer from the Miskitu community of Raiti in Nicaragua, Porcela Sandino, cured dangerous epidemic cases of Grisi Siknis, a mental health illness that affected mainly young women when none of the Western biomedical doctors could do it. Martinez-Cruz explained that the healing principles that guided Porcela Sandino's practice were that of the Pain Iwaia, which includes laman laka (harmony), asla iwaia (living in unity), and the exercise of territorial sovereignty: "Asla iwaia is a guiding principle of collective efforts; it was also identified as the central element for the community to be able to sustain any effort in support of its wellbeing" (181). The chapter also describes how Porcela's healing clashes with Nicaragua's Ministry of Health and the complex hierarchy of knowledge embedded in the Eurocentric narratives of public institutions, constitutive of the "coloniality of power" (175). Even the "intercultural" state exhibits these racist dynamics, as Quijano explains: "the racial axis has a colonial origin and character, but it has proven to be more durable and stable than the colonialism in whose matrix it was established. Therefore, the model of power that is globally hegemonic [i.e., post-Independence] today presupposes an element of coloniality" (Quijano 533).

Mothers of the Land, a film about food sovereignty in the Andes and the role of women as protectors of Indigenous seeds, is discussed in conjunction with food sovereignty issues on Native American reservations. In the fall of 2023, Arapahoe and Paiute film director Tsanavi

Spoonhunter visited CU Boulder to show her documentary *Crow Country: Our Rights to Food Sovereignty* (2022) and discussed with students, faculty, and general audience issues of hunger in reservations and hunting as a Native American right to the land in the Crow reservation in Wyoming. Both films make a powerful comment on the right to practice Indigenous ways of crop growing (*Mothers of the Earth*) and hunting (*Crow Country*), which go against corporate-transgenic production or colonial-state regulations, respectively.

At the end of *Mothers of the Land*, the Indigenous women take the potato seeds to the Svalbard Global Seed Vault in the Norwegian island of Spitsbergen in the Arctic. There, the seeds will be stored and "protected" for future food supply. The end of the film is puzzling. It serves to open up a conversation with students about green colonialism in the Global North and how "conservationist" efforts often come from developed countries that became wealthy by exploiting gas and continue to exploit "green minerals" in Indigenous lands. In the case of the Scandinavian countries, for example, students read an illuminating article about the Sámi, Indigenous peoples from the northern Arctic, who are prohibited from practicing their ancestral reindeer herding because their land is a source of copper: "across the Arctic, many Indigenous people say their way of life is being threatened by a wave of green developments sweeping over their ancestral lands, from wind farms to mines extracting the raw materials for electric vehicles (EVs)." The Sámi say the "green developments" risk disrupting reindeer migration and poisoning fisheries (Day and Worthington).

Environmental Issues and Women Intermediaries: The Language Issue

In the films about the Andes, the predominant language is Quechua, as they are part of a common curricular program with the Quechua classes taught by Doris Loayza[1] at the University of Colorado. In these films, either the directors or scriptwriters or their protagonists are Quechua speakers and members of Indigenous peoples. This selection of material is based on the conviction that language is inseparable from knowledge, cultural practices, and affections; it seeks to give space to the "incommensurability" of Quechua as a language in itself, which becomes accessible only to those who understand and practice Quechua and the philosophy of Sumaq Kawsay. In this sense, the classes seek to restore languages and their knowledge as the primary vehicles of healing, as proposed by McCaslin and Breton:

> Restoring our languages connects us immediately with who we are as peoples. Our languages express the framework for our methods as

peoples by shaping our thoughts, concepts, and ways of interacting. They embody millennia of wisdom gained through experiences, and as a result, our languages reveal ways of responding to harms that are quite different from the colonizers' force-based responses. (24)

Gómez's incorporation of Indigenous language movies, particularly Quechua in this case, works to support a continuous curriculum from Quechua language classes to cultural ones, where students acquire and develop not only language but also cultural competencies. These classes are taken by Indigenous and non-Indigenous students, with different levels of proficiency and interests. As professors we acknowledge that for Indigenous students with Andean ancestors, learning Quechua is a form of language reclamation, especially in the classes of Professor Loayza, who herself is a native Quechua speaker. Additionally, there are students who don't know the language or are not in the process of language reclamation. These students contribute nonetheless to Quechua language revitalization by participating in the program, and our hope is that, by understanding the land land tenure system and coloniality as a root problem, they will also understand the real need for decolonization of the curriculum and their future professions. We have students from different First Nations who decide to take Quechua because it is the only Indigenous language offered for credit at CU Boulder. We also have Chicanx students who take Quechua classes for political affirmation. And we have non-Indigenous students who perceive themselves as allies in the decolonization of the curriculum.

The topic of the incommensurability of language and philosophy raises challenges and questions that are discussed in the course, with particular regard to the role of bilingual Indigenous women as translators and mediators since the first colonial encounters in the Americas. Here, Gómez introduces the first text written in English by an Indigenous woman, Sarah Winnemucca Hopkins, of the Paiute nation, in present-day Nevada. Her book, *Life among the Paiutes*, published in 1887, explores the difficult task carried out by women, who like Nélida (in the *Daughter of the Lake*) and Winnemucca herself, had to translate government documents—and their (unfulfilled) promises—for the other members of their nations. Winnemucca served as an intermediary between the agents of the Malheur and Yakima reservations and the Paiutes in complicated cases that gave rise to violent conflicts, such as the Bannock War (1878).

The book narrates in the first person how Winnemucca carried out her advocacy work for her people from coast to coast in the United States, calling for the return of her people to their ancestral lands at Pyramid Lake in Nevada. Her speeches are highly comparable to those of Nélida in defense of the territories threatened by the Conga mining company. Expropriation, dispossession, military violence, forced displacement, surveillance, and death are in both stories manifested as Western colonial practices on Indigenous territories. Winnemucca's militancy is inserted into the context of the unfulfilled promises of the treaties between Indigenous nations and the U.S. government, making it clear that an essential step for decolonization and the healing of colonial wounds is the recognition that these treaties were based on nation-to-nation agreements, in which the sovereignty of both was recognized. Because treaties attest that Indigenous nations are and have always been sovereign nations, they serve as a signal for present and future decolonization work. Furthermore, because many treaties spell out the boundaries of jurisdiction between Indigenous peoples and modern states, they also spell out who has jurisdiction over whom and under what circumstances. To comply with the colonizers' modus operandi of ignoring these documents as a means of further extending colonial power is to be complicit in the dismantling of native self-determination. The treaties thus speak to the core issue of restorative justice and healing (McCaslin and Breton 25; Robert Clinton 15–33).

The discussion around *Daughter of the Lake* becomes relevant in comparing the territorial problem of the peoples of the Global North and those in the Global South; the dispossession and expropriation of resources continue to be central to local and transnational colonial projects. In "Decolonization Is Not a Metaphor," Tuck and Yang argue that settler colonialism is different from other forms of colonialism in that settlers come with

> the intention of making a new home on the land, a homemaking that insists on settler sovereignty over all things in their new domain. Thus, relying solely on postcolonial literatures or theories of coloniality that ignore settler colonialism will not help to envision the shape that decolonization must take in settler colonial contexts. Within settler colonialism, the most important concern is land/water/air/ subterranean earth (land, for shorthand, in this article). Land is what is most valuable, contested, required. This is both because the settlers make Indigenous land their new home and source of capital, and also because the disruption of Indigenous relationships to land represents a profound epistemic, ontological, cosmological violence. This violence is not temporally contained in the arrival of the settler but is reasserted each day of occupation. (5)

Conga Project, the mining company in *Daughter of the Lake*, is owned by the Minera Yanacocha, a public limited company comprising the Newmont Mining Corporation of Denver (CO), the Buenaventura Mines Company, and the International Financial Corporation (private lending branch of the World Bank), whose share distributions are

51.35%, 43.63%, and 5%, respectively. For this reason, it is impossible to separate the extractive enterprise carried out in Cajamarca (Peru) from the international capital, much of which comes from the United States. In this light, we would like to question the proposal of internal (settler) and external colonialism that Tuck and Yang discuss in their article. The colonialism of the settler who came to make Indigenous lands his home and his business takes on the same form of dispossession and violence in remote lands as well, although not necessarily for the purpose of making these lands home. However, the settler extends networks of extraction and dispossession beyond national borders. In both cases of colonialism, the most important concern is the land/water/air/underground. The land continues to be the most valuable, the most discussed, and the most necessary. Although in external colonialism, Indigenous lands are not the settler's new home, they remain a source of capital; in this way, the rupture of Indigenous relations with the land continues to represent a profound epistemic, ontological, and cosmological violence.

This understanding does not equate all forms of colonialism with settler colonialism. Instead, it shows the land problem as the basis of wealth, power, and law, inside and outside national states, from a transnational perspective. In any case, for this very reason, we agree with Tuck and Yang that "remaining silent on settler colonialism while talking about colonialisms, or tacking on a gesture towards Indigenous people without addressing Indigenous sovereignty or rights, or forwarding a thesis on decolonization without regard to unsettling/de-occupying land, are mistakes" (19).

By this same logic, how can we talk about past and present colonialism in Latin America without recognizing the common history of colonialism in the Americas? Expanding on Tuck and Yang's considerations, it is possible to think of the problem of the immigration of Indigenous peoples from the Global South to the Global North as a problem of colonialism here and there, in connection and linked to each other. This theme is clearly presented in the film *Ixcanul* (2015), directed by Guatemalan Jayro Bustamente. Although most of the actors are Indigenous and the entire film is in Kaqchikel, *Ixcanul* does not fall into the category of Indigenous cinema, given the cultural heterogeneity of its production and circulation. To name just one of the reasons why the film is heterogeneous, the script was initially written in French for a financing contest in France and then translated into Spanish so that the actors, native Kaqchikel speakers, could read and translate it into the film's dialogues. This series of translations forces us to think about the multiple linguistic and cultural negotiations, which undoubtedly resulted in a product as heterogeneous as its process itself and hence the impossibility of calling this film "Indigenous cinema." Something similar happens with the film *Retablo*, as we will see later.

In the analysis of *Ixcanul* in class, Gómez focuses again on the problem of land dispossession, but this time, in connection with forced migration to the north (USA) and the special fragile condition of women. María, the protagonist, is a young Kaqchikel girl in Guatemala who wishes to emigrate to the United States with her boyfriend, José. Her parents, however, have promised her in marriage to the foreman of the land they cultivate to preserve that plot of land that is her family's livelihood. María, obviously, is not happy with this arrangement because she is pregnant by her boyfriend, who abandons her to migrate alone. The problem of the land is at the center of the story as well, especially concerning the coloniality of gender, in the sense that this arranged marriage is the product of a colonial situation.

To complicate matters, the land that María's parents lease from said foreman is infested with snakes, which they have tried to exterminate with chemicals that also come from the United States and have caused even more damage to the land. Nothing seems to be effective in eradicating the snakes, and Maria volunteers to perform a ritual that lands her in the hospital after a snake bites her. At the hospital, the young woman and her family are deceived, as they do not understand Spanish and must trust the interpretation of the foreman, who agrees with the hospital administration to sell María's baby. The long history of the problem of land, its privatization in the hands of foreign capital and wealthy families in Guatemala, and the war conflicts and human rights violations serve as a framework for the problem that arises in the life of a young woman and her family. It is impossible to separate this history from local and global colonialism, and how forced displacement is a product of colonialism. María does not emigrate to the United States, but her daughter does, perhaps—at least that is what María imagines, hoping that the baby will have a better life, evoking the "myth" of immigration to the United States and the American exceptionalism (M. Bianet Castellanos 222–225). The question then is how María's child becomes a "settler" in the United States (as Tuck and Yang would place her) when she is a victim of this same system. Problematizing, then, the links between internal and external colonialism forces us to expand our notions about immigration in colonial situations. As Mailey Blackwell et al. establish in "Critical Latinx Indigeneities":

> Often the racism migrants experience is the entrenched anti-Indian hatred enacted by mestizos and Ladinos as they migrate from Southern Mexico and Central America through Mexico, as well as once they arrive in the United States [...] Indigenous migrants from Latin America are also settlers on other Indigenous peoples' lands, but like Fujikane and Okamura (2008), we also simultaneously deny

The Power of Healing and Indigenizing Feminism in the Classroom 73

that all Indigenous migrants have the political capacity to colonize Northern Native nations. (127)

It is important to acknowledge the complex and multilayered ways of overlapping colonialities experienced by Indigenous migrants across transnational borders (Blackwell 129). Blackwell calls this double hierarchical process "hybrid hegemonies" (2010), to explain, for instance, what happens when many Mayan migrants escaping poverty, land displacement, and state violence in Guatemala are arrested by the U.S. Border Patrol (that have Latinos among their members). These are cases of local, transborder, and hemispheric systems of discrimination and violence against Indigenous peoples. This is not to deny that Indigenous migrants from Latin America arrive on the lands of U.S. Native peoples, on the contrary, but it raises questions such as how to establish relationships of solidarity among Indigenous and Native American peoples, how to use a more complex framework to interpret the settler colonial and colonial structures that have shaped mobility in the region (Castellanos 236), and how indigeneity travel across borders resisting the "assimilation" of Abiayala's Indigenous migrants to the Latinx identity in the United States. As Castellanos ask in "Re-writing the Mexican Immigran narrative": "What do we do we learn about Indigenous women and their migration experiences that speaks to their worldviews, to their ways of being, that goes beyond universalizing discourses of patriarchy, liberation, and assimilation?" (227). These questions will guide the analysis of Indigenous women migration in next iterations of the class.

Indigenous Sexual Dissidence

The film *Retablo* (2017), directed by Álvaro Delgado Aparicio, adds another layer of discussion and analysis to the coloniality of gender and sexuality. This Peruvian film focuses on homophobic violence toward non-heteronormative behaviors in rural Indigenous communities in the Andean highlands. *Retablo*'s production was similar to *Ixcanul*—the director wrote the Spanish script that was translated by the main cast and a team of translators. For this reason, *Retablo* is a bilingual film mostly spoken in Quechua (Chanka variety) and with some sentences in Andean Spanish. The film tells the coming-of-age story of Segundo Paúcar (portrayed by Júnior Béjar), who discovers that his artisan father, Noé (portrayed by Amiel Cayo), is secretly homosexual. When the community discovers this secret as well, they lynch the father and make Segundo the object of bullying by his peers. Noé is subsequently abandoned by this family, who accuse him of being a liar and pervert. The only one who stays by his side is Segundo, who decides to face the social stigma of homosexuality and continue his father's legacy as a artisan of Peruvian. In other words, at the film's end, the adolescent Segundo goes through crucial events in his formation as an adult and popular artist.

Both Gómez and Muñoz-Díaz discuss *Retablo* in their classes, and Muñoz Díaz participated in roundtables about the movie in the Quechua Film Series at CU Boulder. In his upper-division Spanish course, "Latin America in Film," *Retablo* to challenge hegemonic practices in the teaching of the Spanish language and Latin American culture, which often prioritize Hispanic heritage or emphasize discourses on mestizaje and diversity. When discussing *Retablo* with students, Muñoz-Díaz asks them to pay attention to situations where the characters speak either Quechua, Spanish, or both. Although it is beneficial for students to have advanced proficiency in Spanish or Quechua, the success of this method does not depend on proficiency in a second language but on the ability to identify power and status differences in communicative situations. Students may not understand the precise meaning of words, but they grasp the power relations established through them. The aim is to discuss the relationship between Spanish use and the power pattern of coloniality/modernity that explains homophobia.

This methodology challenges the film's message as a call for "tolerance" to explore power dynamics between languages in the Peruvian and Andean contexts. In fact, words like "tolerance," "respect," and "diversity" were used by director Álvaro Delgado Aparicio to advertise the film in the Peruvian commercial circuit ("Álvaro Delgado-Aparicio"). In other words, the discourse of tolerance is the official or authoritative interpretation of the movie. The problem with the tolerance discourse is that it reduces homophobia to an individual issue, where each person freely decides not to discriminate. According to this reading, Segundo's trajectory, from rejecting his father to being the only one who supports him, represents the possibility of a discourse of tolerance that counters homophobia in the Andes. However, even though the film focuses on Segundo's development, his trajectory does not only reveal the main character's journey but also the framework of power in which the sexist and homophobic discourse in the Andes is embedded.

As an important caveat, we do not intend to suggest that Quechua is an ideal or pure language, free from any form of violence and with inherently positive values. Violence, oppression, and colonization can also be exerted in Quechua.[2] Muñoz-Díaz's classes always emphasize that we cannot generalize or essentialize the attributes of languages or their speakers, but rather we must observe how languages and speakers operate with each other in relation to historical dynamics.

Although the main scenes in *Retablo* are spoken in Quechua, Spanish is used in some circumstances that may go unnoticed, given its apparent marginality with respect to the central drama. Among the main Quechua-speaking characters, Noé is the one who consistently uses Spanish. Segundo's father speaks in Spanish with the drivers who offer him rides to the city; with Felícitas (portrayed by Claudia Solís), a mestiza who sells fruits in the market; and with the priest (portrayed by Coco Chiarella), to whom he delivers a retablo on the day Segundo discovers his father's secret sexuality. Likewise, the entire Catholic mass scene is performed in Spanish. On the other hand, although Segundo does not speak Spanish throughout the entire movie, he interacts with other teenagers who speak it while playing soccer at a sports complex. In short, Spanish appears when the main characters venture into external spaces such as the road, the city, the church, the market, and the recreational spaces of the youth. Regarding Segundo's mother, Anatolia (portrayed by Magaly Solier), she never leaves domestic spaces and only appears using Quechua. As mentioned before, Delgado Aparicio's original script did not require that the main characters only use Quechua in the domestic space and Spanish outside of it. In that sense, the diglossia expresses the agency of the actors.

As an example of this proposal for a decolonial reading, *Retablo* begins with a wide shot of a family posing as if waiting to be photographed. It is a lively group chatting animatedly, especially the young women on the left side of the frame. In the middle of the group, the face of Genaro, the head of the family (played by Ubaldo Huamán, a Quechua-speaking actor), shows increasing annoyance. We cannot clearly hear what his noisy family is saying because Segundo's voice-over in Quechua describing the group's clothing overlaps with the ambient sound. As the chatter becomes unbearable for Genaro, he decides to call for order with two shouts in Spanish: "Cuánto más hablan, más nos demoramos" ("The more you talk, the longer we delay") and "Silencio, van a desconcentrar al maestro" ("Silence, you will distract the artist"). Segundo's voice in Quechua is interrupted by these shouts but later returns to continue describing the family group. Finally, the sequence shifts to a reverse shot of Noé covering Segundo's eyes, who has been describing the scene from memory as part of his training to become a retablo artist.

Initially, from a tolerance perspective, the opening sequence presents the connection between Segundo and his father, who trains him to follow in his footsteps as a popular artist. Additionally, Noé covering Segundo's eyes foreshadows the secrets he hides about his sexuality. However, this first scene also opens another line of interpretation based on the use of Spanish as the language of authority over bodies and the repression of sexuality. The character Gerano interrupts a conversation dominated by women with a shout in Spanish. In other words, Spanish is the language of patriarchal authority. The same logic is reproduced in subsequent scenes. The conversation between Noé and the Catholic priest also occurs entirely in Spanish, as does the subsequent mass where Noé takes communion after committing the nefarious sin of homosexuality. The dominant morality that condemns homosexuality is also expressed in Spanish.

On the other hand, in one of the final scenes, when Segundo faces homophobic bullying from his classmates, the insults he receives are entirely in Spanish. The use of Spanish in these scenes might be explained by casting limitations (not all actors are fluent in Quechua), but it also results from conscious decisions by Quechua-speaking actors, such as in the case of Ubaldo Huamán. Additionally, the fact that Felícitas, the object of desire for Segundo and his friend, Mardonio, speaks Spanish gives new meaning to the sexist language and gender violence used by male characters toward her. This is more evident when compared to Anatolia, Segundo's mother: Felícitas is not confined to the domestic space but works in the market selling fruits, and being bilingual, she mainly uses Spanish, the language of authority. In other words, she is a woman who has transcended traditional gender divisions in the Andean "world village" and, therefore, starts occupying traditionally male-dominated spaces. When subordinate masculinity confronts a woman of this kind, its response is to apply corrective violence, as expressed in Mardonio's sexist language and Segundo's attempted assault to her.

Following Muñoz-Díaz's presentation, Gómez's students discuss why some Indigenous and white men collaborate to undermine the power of women and discriminate against homosexual members of their communities. Why are homophobia, machismo, abuse, rape, and other types of violence exerted on Indigenous women and homosexuals by Indigenous men?

In search for responses to that question, students read Argentinean feminist Maria Lugones's "Coloniality of Gender" (a theory built upon Anibal Quijano, Oyèrónkẹ́ Oyěwùmí, and Paula Gunn Allen) and Mapuche weychafe Moira Millán's "Movement of Indigenous Women and Diversities for the Good Living." These readings explain how non-white men were co-opted into the patriarchal roles that the colonial system imposed, disrupting more egalitarian or gynocentric generic systems. Paula Gunn Allen argues that many Native American tribes were matriarchal, recognized more than two genders, regarded "third" gendering and homosexuality positively, and understood gender in egalitarian terms rather than in the terms of subordination that Euro-centered capitalism imposed on them (qtd. in Lugones 199). Allen enables us to see that the scope of the gender differentials was much more encompassing since it did not rest on biology.[3]

In Maria Lugones's view, one of the first achievements of the colonial state was the creation of "women" as a category (202). At one level, the transformation of state power into male power was achieved by excluding women from government.[4] Addressing Anibal Quijano's coloniality of power, Lugones cites Oyèrónkẹ́ Oyèwùmí (in the case of Yoruba colonization), recognizing two crucial colonization processes: the imposition of races with the consequent inferiorization of non-white, and the inferiorization of anafemales. The latter spread very widely through various practices, ranging from exclusion from leadership roles to loss of land ownership and other significant economic consequences. Replacing gynecocratic spiritual plurality with a male supreme being, as Christianity did, was crucial in subduing the tribes. Lugones, following Paula Gunn Allen, argues that the passage of Indigenous tribes from egalitarian and gynecratic to hierarchical and patriarchal required the fulfillment of several objectives, among which were that the primacy of the female as creator be displaced and replaced by male creators and that people be "driven from their lands, deprived of their economic livelihood, and forced to diminish or abandon every enterprise on which their subsistence, philosophy, and ritual system depend. Already dependent on white institutions for their survival, tribal systems cannot maintain gynecracy when patriarchy—indeed their survival—requires male domination" (Allen qtd. in Lugones, 199).

The coloniality of gender is linked to the expropriation of land to the extent that the colonial system gave men the authority to obtain, inherit, and sell land to the detriment of women. U.S. settler colonialism, through several Federal Indian Policy Acts—such as the Dawes Act (1887), the Indian Reorganization Act (1934), and Indian Relocation Act (1956)—imposed heteronormativity and Christian monogamy, redefining sexual practices, familiar structures, and gender norms and power dynamics in Indigenous societies, with the goal of assimilating them to Western values and capitalism. The Dawes Act redistributed the land in lots and established that only the male heads of households and nuclear families would own the land and become citizens. The Reorganization Act mirrored the U.S. government system in tribal government, again favoring the men by giving them a position of power. The Relocation Act forced Indigenous peoples to move to urban settings where the hierarchical workforce was split between breadwinners (men) and domestic laborers (women).[5]

Another example studied in the class is that of the Argentine colonial state. In 1869, the Argentine Civil Code (enacted in 1871) clarified the rights of male heads of households. In classifying both women and children as minors, this code reiterated a husband's authority over his wife and his responsibility to provide for her. It also required a woman to obtain her husband's permission before she could initiate any legal action, such as that needed to buy, sell, or mortgage property; become employed; or administer her own wages. As a consequence of this code, polygamy and other forms of sexuality quickly became a target of Argentine efforts to integrate Indigenous people. The state instituted repressive measures to prohibit marriage with two or more women, as well as other tribal ceremonies that offended "moral decency" (Kerr, Ashley, *Sex, Skulls and Citizenship* 31). This is, in part, why Moira Millán, the founder of the Women and Diversities Movement for Good Living in Argentina, has defined the struggle of Indigenous women outside of Western feminism. In her view, unlike Western feminism, Indigenous women's resistance has always been anti-colonial because the anti-patriarchal struggle is an anti-colonial struggle.

Conclusion

Hearing stories of colonization by Indigenous peoples is where healing begins. Gómez's class aims to create a space for attentive listening and reflection. Students are asked to listen to the stories told by Indigenous women in their own languages in these films and texts, following the Mapuche practice of alkütun, which involves active, attentive listening in a manner that opens the ear, body, and mind to a process of learning.

The class then becomes a forum for Indigenous peoples to tell what has happened to them during colonization and make visible the painful reality of past and present colonialism. As stated in the introduction, a mere inclusion of Indigenous languages and cultures is not enough to dismantle oppression. For profound healing, it is imperative to start naming the root harm of colonialism and land dispossession. Acknowledging Indigenous land means fighting the colonial structures of power, gender, sexuality, economy, knowledge, and being. In Gómez's class design, material selection, and discussion, students constantly ask themselves if they engage in this transformation by naming local and global colonialism, establishing comparative frameworks of decolonization and transnational solidarities.

Thus, the class aims to follow McCaslin and Breton's call for land return, reparations, restitution, adherence to treaties, and hence the return of sovereign jurisdiction homelands: "Decolonizing is not just a big word; it is the core of healing justice for Indigenous peoples" (29). Furthermore, Gómez's class follows Keme's proposal of Abiayala as a locus of enunciation whence to imagine Indigenous pluriversality and hemispheric land reclamation against Western (white and criollo-mestizo) imposition of national borders, as they are constitutive of the ethnocentric and colonial logic of the nation-states (53).

Notes

1 The bio information of Doris Loayza is provided in note 47.
2 Accusations of human rights violations weigh upon current Peruvian President Dina Boluarte, the first Quechua-speaking woman to assume this position and the first to use Quechua in official speeches. Since assuming office in mid-December 2021, about 50 Peruvians from Ayacucho and Puno have been murdered by the repressive forces of the state. Dina Boluarte's use of Quechua is "theatrical" (pretentious, superficial) due to her absolute lack of commitment to the communities that use this language on a daily basis. It is also reminiscent to the Quechua spoken by gamonales, the old Andean landowning class that, while sharing cultural traits with Quechua-speaking Indigenous people, subjected them to a brutal regime of exploitation.
3 Michael J. Horswell comments usefully on the term "third gender": "The 'third' is emblematic of other possible combinations than the dimorphic" (qtn in Lugones 201). In other words, it does not mean that there are three genders; it is instead a way of breaking with the sex and gender bipolarity.
4 In her book *The Invention of Women*, Oyèwùmí maintains that the system of gender oppression that European colonialism imposed on the Yorubas covered all aspects of women's lives, not just reproduction. Oyèwùmí maintains that before colonialism in Yoruba society, there was no such division of labor according to gender. The anatomically female (anafemale) and the anatomically male (anamale) did not have fixed roles in government or public life, for example. The hierarchical gender system did not exist. The different positions occupied by anafemales or anamales were much more interchangeable and flexible. With the advent of colonialism, the inferiorization of Africans widely extended the inferiorization of anafemales, excluding them from leadership roles and causing them to lose ownership over land and other important economic domains. Argentinean anthropologist Rita Segato reaches a similar conclusion: indeed, non-white men were co-opted, but because there already existed a favorable terrain—that is, the possibility for such co-option within a low-intensity patriarchy—prior to the colonial intrusion. Therefore, Segato's main criticism of Lugones and Oyèwùmí is that although the gender system of the Yorubas was more flexible, the female gender already existed in an unequal distribution of social power, which she calls "low intensity patriachy" (Segato 69).
5 See also Tallbear, "Feminist, Queer, and Indigenous Thinking," and Tallbear and Willey, "Critical Relationality."

Epilogue

The Quechua Language Program at the University of Colorado, Boulder

Leila Gómez

Teaching Indigenous languages is at the core of decolonizing education. One of our priorities is to generate support for the survival, reclamation, and revitalization of Indigenous languages of Abiayala. The Latin American and Latinx Studies Center (LALSC) at the University of Colorado started this decolonizing project with the creation of Quechua classes, thanks to federal grants, called "Undergraduate International Studies Foreign Languages" (UISFL). Creating a Quechua language program implied institutional efforts, with successes and challenges, that required the support of many actors with solid determination. The first and most important step was to hire a native Quechua instructor who could design the curriculum and teach not only the language but also the culture and the worldview of Quechua speakers. The second step was the development of specialized teaching materials for Quechua instruction at institutions of higher education, and ensuring that those materials were accessible to English-speaking students who might not necessarily speak Spanish. The third step was establishing and enhancing an interdisciplinary curriculum with expanded course offerings, study abroad opportunities, and event planning so that it better supported underrepresented students and Colorado's growing Latinx Indigenous population.

We knew that to create a strong program, we needed our Quechua classes to satisfy a graduation requirement. Students can now fulfill the College of Arts and Sciences' core requirement of foreign language by completing a sequence of three Quechua classes. The university's official recognition has thus elevated the status of our Quechua program and put it on equal footing with other foreign language programs at the university. Quechua, the most widely spoken Indigenous language in the Americas, is now the first Indigenous language to satisfy the college's foreign language requirement. At the University of Colorado, to fulfill the foreign language requirement of the College of Arts and Sciences, classes need to be taught up to the intermediate level; therefore, we offer QUEC 1010 Beginner 1, QUEC 1020 Beginner 2, and QUEC 2110 Intermediate 1. These classes have been designed and taught by Doris Loayza,[1] and they are coordinated by Leila Gómez, director of the program.[2]

Developing teaching materials was also at the heart of the project. No textbook that includes all the Quechua variants in the Southern Andes has ever been created for Quechua language instruction. With UISFL funding, we have been supporting the QINTI group of Quechua consultants, linguists, and educators, led by Carlos Molina-Vidal, who are all working on a multimedia textbook that will make Quechua instruction more feasible and effective for both language learners and teachers in Colorado and across the United States. The QINTI group has been meeting periodically to work together on grammar explanations, audio recordings, practice exercises, etc. The QINTI textbook incorporates the Quechua variants from Peru, Bolivia, and Northern Argentina and will be trilingual (in Quechua, Spanish, and English).

Moreover, the CU Quechua program comprises not only language classes but also interdisciplinary, cultural, and study-abroad classes. Students taking the Quechua classes benefit from enrolling in cultural content classes such as "Geography of the Andes," "Introduction to Latin American and Latinx Studies," and "Gender and Indigeneity in Film and Literature of the Americas" (discussed in Chapter 4), in which they familiarize themselves with Andean and other Indigenous worldviews, as well as the Western colonization of the land through history, literature, and film. These classes seek to create liberating and decolonizing spaces for Indigenous and non-Indigenous students and focus on the examination of colonial past and present, settler colonialism, land dispossession, and cultural genocide (Shirley 9).

A partnership with the university libraries has resulted in new collections of books and films in other Indigenous languages (in addition to Quechua) (as discussed in Chapters 1 and 2), which have helped to enrich this curriculum. The Quechua program also supports students who are interested in traveling abroad to study or practice any Indigenous languages or carry out projects connected to any Indigenous languages of the Americas.

As explained in Chapter 4, we have a host of Indigenous students engaged in a conscientious process of language reclamation, from those who were not taught Quechua by their grandparents or immigrant parents, to students from different First Nations who decide to take Quechua because it is the only Indigenous language of the Americas offered for course credit at CU-Boulder. We have Chicanx students who take Quechua as a political affirmation of their bond with the Indigenous land of their ancestors. And we have non-Indigenous students, who perceive themselves as allies in the decolonization of the curriculum. All of them contribute greatly to the language revitalization.

Moreover, to maintain a vibrant program, it is fundamental to engage in the recruitment and retention of students through intense academic and cultural event programming that extends beyond the University of Colorado to national and international contexts with artists, scholars, and professionals from Abiayala. The Quechua program organizes film series, guest lectures, game nights, and week-long conferences such as the Celebrating the Indigenous Americas Week, with virtual and in-person events focusing on the contribution and presence of Latin American Indigenous languages, cultures, politics, science, and arts. Panels and roundtables have addressed topics such as food sovereignty, bilingual education, social movements, land reclamation, migration, environmental justice, university-community partnerships, broadcasting and communication, and many more. We have also invited audiences to join us for hip-hop concerts, poetry readings, cooking lessons, film screenings, and various other events.

Celebrating the Indigenous Americas provides a space for a south-north exchange of ideas and knowledge, fosters intercontinental dialogue, and imagines and creates hemispheric alliances—e.g., the QINTI textbook now includes the support of the UISFL grant in Colorado. We can, thanks to the work of interpreters, transcend linguistic barriers and, potentially, embrace transhemispheric projects. These events and the Quechua Program at large are redefining the cultural capital of our students. As Herlihy-Mera reminds us:

> The democratization of cultural capital in the discipline not only lies on the canon and its expansion, it also lies on new emphases, new sources, new voices—each of which can emerge from pedagogies imbued with critical integration of non-imperial sensibilities cultivated by students [and faculty] in their own languages, communities and cultures. (Herlihy-Mera 52)

Contrary to projects that conceive a "global Indigeneity" from the geographical contexts demarcated by an Anglophone colonial-linguistic genealogy—which exhibits what Victoria Bomberry explained as "myopic focus within what is today the United States and Canada" and "replicates colonial constructs, including the othering of Indigenous peoples from south of the U.S.-Mexico border" (213 quoted in Keme, p. 47)—the Quechua Program proposes a hemispheric, non-imperial critical view of Indigeneity, one that takes Abiayala and its more than thousand Indigenous languages as loci of enunciation.

Notes

1 Doris Loayza is a native Quechua and Spanish speaker, educator, and multimedia producer from Peru. She grew up in Llamellin, Ancash in the Peruvian Andes, and earned a B.A. in psychology from the Universidad Nacional Mayor de San Marcos in Lima. In 2007, she moved to New York City, and in 2014, earned an M.A. in Latin American & Caribbean studies from NYU, where she helped organize Andean cultural activities and produced a Quechua language podcast. After graduating, Doris studied documentary storytelling at the Bronx Documentary Center and made a short film, "Bronx Llaktamanta," about a Kichwa radio show in New York that was featured at the United Nations, universities, and other venues. Since 2021, she has taught Quechua and Latin American studies classes at the University of Colorado, Boulder.

2 Leila Gómez is a professor of women and gender studies at the University of Colorado, Boulder and principal investigator of the UISFL grant. She started the Quechua Program during her time as director of the Latin American and Latinx Studies Center (LALSC) at CU Boulder from 2017 to 2023. She is the author of *Impossible Domesticity: Travels in Mexico* (Pittsburgh UP, 2021) and several other books. In 2020, she was selected as editor of the ELN special Issue: Indigenous Narratives of Origin and Land Reclamation 58(1) 2020. In 2020 and 2022, Gómez received two consecutive U.S. Department of Education UISFL grants to develop the Quechua program at CU Boulder, which has been in place since 2021. Gómez's recent research focuses on documentaries and films on land issues and environmental justice by Latin American women filmmakers. She is also PI of the Seed Grant "Global Indigeneity and Land Struggle: Documentary Film for Sustainable Futures" offered by CU Boulder in partnership with Marquette University, the University of Konstanz, and Colby College.

Works Cited

Allen, Paula Gunn. *The Sacred Hoop: Recovering the Feminine in American Indian Tradition*. Beacon Press, 1986.

"Álvaro Delgado-Aparicio: 'Retablo es un llamado urgente a la tolerancia.'" *La República*, 16 Apr. 2019, https://larepublica.pe/cultural/1451380-retablo-llamado-urgente-tolerancia.

Álvarez Ccoscco, Irma. "Bringing It Home 02: National Museum of the American Indian." *Smithsonian Institution*, 10 Dec. 2014, https://www.si.edu/object/yt_OfDgRhDmyk.

Álvarez Ccoscco, Irma. "Kawsaq." *Musuq Illa*, 2021, https://musuqilla.info/harawikuna-qulqakuna/kawsaq/.

Álvarez Ccoscco, Irma. "Poetry Reading." *Celebrating the Indigenous Americas*, 5 Mar. 2021, University of Colorado Boulder.

"Amazon Reported that Kindle ebook Sales Have Officially Surpassed Sales of Print Books." *Information Today*, vol. 28, no. 7, Jul.–Aug. 2011, p. 12, https://link.gale.com/apps/doc/A260874188/CDB?u=coloboulder&sid=bookmark-CDB&xid=b7c271a9.

Andrade Ciudad, Luis, Rosaleen Howard, and Raquel de Pedro Ricoy. "Activismo, derechos lingüísticos e ideologías: la traducción e interpretación en lenguas originarias en el Perú." *INDIANA -Anthropologische Studien zu Lateinamerika und der Karibik*, vol. 35, no. 1, Aug. 2018, pp. 139–163, 10.18441/ind.v35i1.139-163.

Argentina, Ministerio de Cultura. "Convocatoria para la Feria del Libro sobre Pueblos Originarios." *Argentina.gob.ar*, 17 Jul. 2023, https://www.argentina.gob.ar/noticias/convocatoria-para-la-feria-del-libro-sobre-pueblos-originarios.

Arguedas, José María. *The Fox from Up-Above and the Fox from Down-Below*. Translated by Frances Horning Barraclough, Pittsburgh UP, 2000.

Ash, Timothy, Jesus Ignacio Cardozo, Hortensia Cabellero, and Jose Bortoli. "The Story We Now Want to Hear Is Not Ours to Tell: Relinquishing Control Over Representation: Toward Sharing Visual Communication Skills with the Yanomami." *Visual Anthropology Review* vol. 7, no. 2, Fall 1991, pp. 102–106.

Association of College & Research Libraries. "Academic Libraries." American Library Association, https://www-ala-org.colorado.idm.oclc.org/educationcareers/libcareers/type/academic.

Benson, Carol, and Kimmo Kosonen. *Language Issues in Comparative Education: Inclusive Teaching and Learning in Non-Dominant Languages and Cultures*. Sense Publishers, 2013, 10.1007/978-94-6209-218-1.

Blackwell, Maylei. "Lideres Campesinas: Nepantla Strategies and Grassroots Organizing at the Intersection of Gender and Globalization." *Aztlan: A Journal of Chicano Studies*, vol. 35, 2010, pp. 13–47.

Blackwell, Maylei, Floridalma Boj Lopez, and Luis Urrieta Jr. "Special Issue: Critical Latinx Indigeneities." *Latino Studies*, vol. 15, no. 2, 2017, pp. 126–137, 10.1057/s41276-017-0064-0.

Blaser, Mario, and Marisol de la Cadena. "Introduction. Pluriverse. Proposal for a World of Many Worlds." *A World of Many Worlds*, edited by Marisol De la Cadena and Mario Blaser, Duke UP, 2018.

Borges, Toine, and Vivien Petras. "An In-Depth Analysis of Tags and Controlled Metadata for Books Search." *iConference 2017 Proceedings*, vol. 2, 2017, pp. 15–30, 10.977617004.

"Braiding Sweetgrass: Indigenous Wisdom, Scientific Knowledge, and the Teaching of Plants." LibraryThing, https://www.librarything.com/work/30375223.

Breuer, Esther Odilia, and Elke van Steendam. "Multiple Approaches to Understanding and Working with Multilingual (Multi-) Literacy." *Multilingual Literacy*, edited by Esther Odilia Breuer, Eva Lindgren, Anat Stavans, and Elke Van Steendam, Multilingual Matters, 2021, pp. 1–18.

Brooks, Sam. "Introduction: The Importance of Open Communication Between Libraries and Vendors." *Library/Vendor Relationships*, edited by Sam Brooks and David H. Carlson, Routledge, 2012, pp. 1–4.

Cabán, Pedro. *Borderless Borders: U.S. Latinos, Latin Americans, and the Paradox of Interdependence*, edited by Frank Bonilla, Temple UP, 2009, pp. 195–215.

Castellanos, M. Bianet. "Rewriting the Mexican Immigrant Narrative: Situating Indigeneity in Maya Women's Stories." *Latino Studies*, vol. 15, no. 2, 2017, pp. 219–241, 10.1057/s41276-017-0057-z.

Castro-Klarén, Sara. "Notes from the Field: Decolonizing the curriculum/The 'Spanish' Major." *Decolonial Approaches to Latin American Literatures and Cultures*, edited by Juan G. Ramos and Tara Daly, Palgrave Macmillan, 2016, pp. 3–18.

Clark, Giles N., and Angus Phillips. *Inside Book Publishing*. Sixth edition, Routledge, 2020.

Clinton, Robert. "Treaties with Native Nations." *Nation to Nation: Treaties between the United States & American Indian Nations*, edited by Suzan Shown Harjo, National Museum of the American Indian, Smithsonian Books, 2014, pp.15–33.

Coe, George. "Managing Customer Relationships: A Book Vendor Point-of-View." *Journal of Library Administration*, vol. 44, no. 3–4, Aug. 2006, pp. 43–55, 10.1300/J111v44n03_05.

Colchado Lucio, Óscar. *Kuya kuya: el cuento más bello sobre el amor andino*. Editorial San Marcos, 2019.

Collins, Amy. "The Differences between Book Wholesalers and Distributors." *Author Learning Center*, https://www.authorlearningcenter.com/publishing/distribution-sales/w/booksellers/7151/the-differences-between-book-wholesalers-and-distributors.

Collins, Amy. *The Write Way: Everything You Need to Know about Publishing, Selling and Marketing Your Book*. New Shelves Books, 2015.

Collyer, Fran. "Global Patterns in the Publishing of Academic Knowledge: Global North, Global South." *Current Sociology*, vol. 66, Nov. 2016, pp. 56–73.

Comajoan-Colomé, Llorenç, and Serafín M. Coronel-Molina. "What Does Language Revitalisation in the Twenty-First Century Look Like? New Trends and Frameworks." *Journal of Multilingual and Multicultural Development*, vol. 42, no. 10, Nov. 2021, pp. 897–904, 10.1080/01434632.2020.1827643.

Convocatoria Premio Cuento Joven UNAM-SECTEI 2023. Libros UNAM, 2023, https://www.libros.unam.mx/convocatoriaPremioCuentoJoven_UNAM-SECTEI-2023.pdf.

Day, Lauren, and Anne Worthington. "A Voice for the Arctic. A Wave of 'Green Colonisation' Is Threatening an Indigenous People's Way of Life in the Arctic. Can Having a Voice to Parliament Save It?" *ABC News*, 9 Oct. 2022, https://www.abc.net.au/news/2.

De la Cadena, Marisol. "Are 'Mestizos' Hybrids? The Conceptual Politics of Andean Identities." *Journal of Latin American Studies*, vol. 37, pp. 259–284, https://www.jstor.org/stable/3875686.

Doherty, John J. "The Academic Librarian and the Hegemony of the Canon." *Journal of Academic Librarianship*, vol. 24, Sep. 1998, pp. 403–406.

Echeverría, Andrea. "Mapurbe Identity and Admapu in David Aniñir's Poetry." *Bulletin of Latin American Research*, vol. 38, no. 2, 2019, pp. 208–221, 10.1111/blar.12838.

Echeverría, Andrea. "Three Mapunky Poems: David Aniñir Guilitraro – Siwar Mayu." *Siwar Mayu: A River of Hummingbirds*, https://siwarmayu.com/three-mapunky-poems-david-aninir-guilitraro/.

Falconí Trávez, Diego. *From Ashes to Text: Andean Literature of Sexual Dissidence in the 20th Century*. Translated by Carrie Hamilton, Polity Press, 2022.

Fernando, Chrisantha, Rhtta-Liisa Valijärvi, and Rcichard A. Goldstein. "A Model of the Mechanisms of Language Extinction and Revitalization Strategies to Save Endangered Languages." *Human Biology*, vol. 82, no. 1, 2010, pp. 47–75, 10.3378/027.082.0104.

Fúnez-Flores, Jairo I. "Anibal Quijano: (Dis)Entangling the Geopolitics and Coloniality of Curriculum." *Curriculum Journal*, 2023, 10.1002/curj.219.

Gantt, Amy M. "Native Language Revitalization: Keeping the Languages Alive and Thriving." *Native Leadership: Past, Present, and Future*, edited by Mark B. Spencer, Southeastern Oklahoma State University, 2016, pp. 13–19, https://www.se.edu/native-american/wp-content/uploads/sites/49/2019/09/AAA-NAS-2015-Proceedings-Gantt.pdf.

Gómez, Leila. "Introduction." *English Language Notes*, vol. 58, no. 1, Apr. 2020, pp. 1–8, 10.1215/00138282-8237366.

Gómez, Leila. "Moira Millán on Land Struggle and Terricidio." *ASAP Journal*, 25 Sep. 2023, https://asapjournal.com/geosemantics-moira-millan-on-land-struggle-and-terricidio-leila-gomez/.

Goodwin, Cathy. "The E-Duke Scholarly Collection: E-Book v. Print Use." *Collection Building*, vol. 33, no. 4, Sep. 2014, pp. 101–105, 10.1108/CB-05-2014-0024.

Guamán Poma de Ayala, Felipe. "Native Administrators of Resources (815–815) [814]: Guaman Poma, Nueva corónica y buen gobierno (1615)." *Royal Danish Library*, https://poma.kb.dk/permalink/2006/poma/814/en/text/?open=idm562

Guan, Shu-Sha A., Patricia M Greenfield, and Marjorie F Orellana. "Translating into Understanding: Language Brokering and Prosocial Development in Emerging Adults from Immigrant Families." *Journal of Adolescent Research*, vol. 29, May 2014, pp. 331–355.

Guillory, John. *Cultural Capital: The Problem of Literary Canon Formation/John Guillory*. The Chicago UP, 2007.

Gustafson, Ried. "Hetero-patriarchy and Settler Colonialism." *YouTube*, uploaded by TEDx Talks, 26 Apr. 2019, https://www.youtube.com/watch?v=-wRbfOmHgts.

Hanson, Aubrey Jean. *Literatures, Communities, and Learning: Conversations with Indigenous Writers*. Wilfrid Laurier UP, 2020.
Herlihy-Mera, Jeffrey. *Decolonizing American Spanish: Eurocentrism and Foreignness in the Imperial Ecosystem*. Pittsburgh UP, 2022.
Hobart, Elizabeth. "Recording Creator Characteristics for Native American Authors: An Analysis of Bibliographic Records." *Cataloging & Classification Quarterly*, vol. 58, no. 1, 2020, pp. 59–75. 10.1080/01639374.2019.1704333.
Hoffman, Gretchen L. "Meeting Users' Needs in Cataloging: What Is the Right Thing to Do?" *Cataloging & Classification Quarterly*, vol. 47, no. 7, 2009, pp. 631–641. 10.1080/01639370903111999.
Hopkins, Sarah Winnemucca. *Life Among the Piutes: Their Qrongs and Laims*, edited by Mary Tyler Peabody Mann, Nevada UP, 1994 [1883].
Horswell, Michael J. "Toward and Andean Theory of Ritual Same-Sex Sexuality and Third-Gender Subjectivity." *Infamous Desire: Male Homosexuality in Colonial Latin America*, edited by Peter Herman Sigal, Chicago UP, 2003, pp. 25–69.
"How Publishing Works." Publishers Association, https://www.publishers.org.uk/about-publishing/how-publishing-works/.
Ibacache, Kathia, Javier Munoz-Diaz, Caitlin M. Berry, and Eric A. Vance. "Forgotten Hispano-American Literature: Representation of Hispano-American Presses in Academic Libraries." *College & Research Libraries*, vol. 81, no. 6, Sep. 2020, pp. 928–944, 10.5860/crl.81.6.928.
"In Memoriam: Remembering 52 Indigenous Defenders Who Were Murdered in 2022 in Latin America." *Cultural Survival*, 26 Feb. 2023, https://www.culturalsurvival.org/news/memoriam-remembering-52-indigenous-defenders-who-were-murdered-2022-latin-america.
"Inauguran la Feria Regional del Libro en Lenguas Indígenas (FERELLI 2022)." *La Onda Oaxaca*, 12 Oct. 2022, https://www.laondaoaxaca.com.mx/2022/10/inauguran-la-feria-regional-del-libro-en-lenguas-indigenas-ferelli-2022/.
Ixcanul. Directed by Jayro Bustamante, Guatemala, 2015.
Jaffee, Annie, and Zachary A. Casey. "Settler Colonialism." *Encyclopedia of Critical Whiteness Studies in Education*, edited by Zachary A. Casey, Brill Sense, 2021.
Jezewski, Mary Ann. "Culture Brokering in Migrant Farmworker Health Care." *Western Journal of Nursing Research*, vol. 12, no. 4, 1990, pp. 497–513, 10.1177/019394599001200406.
Keme, Emil. "For Abiayala to Live, the Americas Must Die: Toward a Transhemispheric Indigeneity." *Native American and Indigenous Studies*, translated by Adam Coon, vol. 5, no. 1, 2018, pp. 42–68, 10.5749/natiindistudj.5.1.0042.
Kerr, Ashley. *Sex, Skulls, and Citizenship*. Vanderbilt UP, 2020.
Kimmerer, Robin Wall. *Braiding Sweetgrass: Indigenous Wisdom, Scientific Knowledge, and the Teaching of Plants*. First edition, Milkweed Editions, 2013.
"La institución." *Real Academia Española*, https://www.rae.es/la-institucion.
Lakhani, Nina. "Who Killed Berta Cáceres? Behind the Brutal Murder of an Environment Crusader." *The Guardian*, 2 Jun. 2020, https://www.theguardian.com/world/2020/jun/02/who-killed-berta-caceres-behind-the-brutal-of-an-environment-crusader.
Lamb, Terry. "Towards a Plurilingual Habitus: Engendering Interlinguality in Urban Spaces." *International Journal of Pedagogies and Learning*, vol. 10, no. 2, May 2015, pp. 151–165, 10.1080/22040552.2015.1113848.
Latour, Bruno. *Science in Action: How to Follow Scientists and Engineers through Society*. Open UP, 1987.

Lempert, William. "Telling Their Own Stories: Indigenous Film as Critical Identity Discourse." *The Applied Anthropologist*, vol. 32, no. 1, 2012, pp. 23–32.
Leonard, Wesley Y. "Producing Language Reclamation by Decolonizing 'Language.'" *Language Documentation and Description*, vol. 14, Dec. 2017, 10.25894/ldd146.
Leonard, Wesley Y. "Telling Their Own Stories: Indigenous Film As Critical Identity Discourse." *The Applies Anthropologist*, vol. 32, no. 1, 2012, pp. 23–32.
Lewis, Simon L., and Mark A. Maslin. "Defining the Anthropocene." *Nature*, vol. 519, no. 7542, 2015, pp. 171–7580, 10.1038/nature14258.
Lugones, Maria. "Heterosexualism and the Colonial/Modern Gender System." *Hypatia*, vol. 22, no. 1, 2007, pp. 186–209.
Majluf, Natalia. *Inventing Indigenism: Francisco Laso's Image of Modern Peru*. First edition, Texas UP, 2021.
Mama Irene, Healer of the Andes. Directed by Elisabeth Mohlmann, Peru, Germany, 2022.
Mariátegui, José Carlos. *Seven Interpretive Essays on Peruvian Reality*. Translated by Marjory Urquidi. University of Texas Press, 1971.
Marshall, E. Anne. "Integrating Indigenous and Traditional Practices in Refugee Mental Health Therapy." *Refugee Mental Health*, edited by Jamie D. Aten and Jenny Hwang, American Psychological Association, 2021, pp. 281–302.
Martínez-Cruz, Jessica. "This Knowledge Counts! Harmony and Spirituality in Miskitu Critical Thought." *Decolonial Feminism in Abya Yala Caribbean, Meso, and South American Contributions and Challenges*, edited by Yuderkys Espinosa Miñoso, Maria Lugones, and Nelson Maldonado-Torres, Rowman and Littlefield Publishers, 2022.
Mbembe, Achille Joseph. "Decolonizing the University: New Directions." *Arts and Humanities in Higher Education*, vol. 15, no. 1, Feb. 2016, pp. 29–45, 10.1177/1474022215618513.
McCaslin, Wanda D., and Denise C. Breton. "Justice as Healing: Going Outside the Colonizers' Cage." *Handbook of Critical and Indigenous Methodologies*, SAGE Publications, 2008, pp. 511–530. 10.4135/9781483385686.
Mendoza-Mori, Américo. "Quechua Language Programs in the United States: Cultural Hubs for Indigenous Cultures." *Chiricú Journal: Latina/o Literatures, Arts, and Cultures*, vol. 1, no. 2, 2017, pp. 43–55.
Mendoza-Mori, Américo, and Rachel Sprouse. "Hemispheric Quechua: Language Education and Reclamation within Diasporic Communities in the United States." *International Journal of the Sociology of Language*, vol. 2023, no. 280, Mar. 2023, pp. 135–142, 10.1515/ijsl-2022-0024.
Mignolo, Walter D. "Capitalism and Geopolitics of Knowledge: Latin American Social Thought and Latino American Studies." *Critical Latin American and Latino Studies*, edited by Juan Poblete, University of Minnesota Press, 2003, pp. 32–75.
Minnesota Historical Society. "Gift-Giving Practices." *Snake River Fur Post*, https://www.mnhs.org/furpost/learn/gift-giving.
Moore, Jason W. *Anthropocene or Capitalocene?: Nature, History, and the Crisis of Capitalism*. PM Press, 2016.
Morales, Alejandro, and William E. Hanson. "Language Brokering: An Integrative Review of the Literature." *Hispanic Journal of Behavioral Sciences*, vol. 27, 2005, pp. 471–503.
Mothers of the Land. Directed by Diego Sarmiento and Santiago Sarmiento, Peru, 2020.

Nadarajah, Yaso, and Adam Grydehøj. "Island Studies as a Decolonial Project." *Island Studies Journal*, vol. 11, no. 2, 2016, pp. 437–446, https://doaj.org/article/4657ddfdd0a241f1a5510225386a7008.

National Center for Cultural Competence. "What is the Role of Cultural Brokers in Health Care Delivery." *Bridging the Cultural Divide in Health Care Settings: The Essential Role of Cultural Broker Programs*, 2004, https://nccc.georgetown.edu/documents/Cultural_Broker_Guide_English.pdf.

Niño, Yeisi Julieth. "Graciela Huinao y la poesía mapuche: la frontera como marca." *Revista de Teoría y Crítica de Poesía Latinoamericana*, vol. 7, no. 12, 2020, pp. 88–103, https://fh.mdp.edu.ar/revistas/index.php/eljardindelospoetas/article/view/5369.

On the Record. Library of Congress Working Group on the Future of Bibliographic Control, 9 Jan. 2008, https://www.loc.gov/bibliographic-future/news/lcwg-ontherecord-jan08-final.pdf.

Oyěwùmí, Oyèrónké. *The Invention of Women: Making an African Sense of Western Gender Discourses*. Minnesota UP, 1997.

Past, Ámbar, Xalik Guzmán Bakbolom, and Petra Hernándes. *Conjuros y ebriedades: cantos de mujeres mayas*. Taller Leñateros, 1997.

Petitt, Karl, and Erin Elzi. "Unsettling the Library Catalog: A Case Study in Reducing the Presence of 'Indians of North America' and Similar Subject Headings." *Library Resources & Technical Services*, vol. 67, no. 2, 2023, 10.5860/lrts.67n2.4.

Poblete, Juan. "Introduction". *Critical Latin American and Latino Studies*, Minnesota UP, 2003, pp. ix–xli.

Q.ai. "What Companies Are Fueling the Progress in Natural Language Processing? Moving This Branch of AI Past Translators and Speech-To-Text". *Forbes*, 6 Feb. 2023, https://www.forbes.com/sites/qai/2023/02/06/what-companies-are-fueling-the-progress-in-natural-language-processing-moving-this-branch-of-ai-past-translators-and-speech-to-text/?sh=ad9ab6b4a8ff.

"¿Quiénes somos?" Pehuén Editores, https://tienda.pehuen.cl/pages/quienes-somos.

Quijano, Anibal. "Coloniality of Power, Eurocentrism, and Latin America." *Nepantla: Views from South*, vol. 1, 2000, pp. 533–580.

Ramírez Zavala, Ana Luz. "Indio/Indígena, 1750–1850." *Historia Mexicana*, vol. 60, no. 3 (239), 2011, pp. 1643–1681, https://www.jstor.org/stable/41151295.

Ramos, Juan G., and Tara Daly. "Introduction: Decolonial Strategies for Reading and Looking with and against the Grain." *Decolonial Approaches to Latin American Literatures and Cultures*, edited by Juan G. Ramos and Tara Daly, Palgrave Macmillan, 2016, pp. xiii–xxxvi.

Rivera Cusicanqui, Silvia. "Ch'ixinakax utxiwa: A Reflection on the Practices and Discourses of Decolonization." *South Atlantic Quarterly*, vol. 111, no. 1, 2012, pp. 95–109. 10.1215/00382876-1472612.

Rivera Cusicanqui, Silvia. "Un mundo ch'ixi es posible: Memoria, mercado y colonialism." *Un mundo ch'ixi es posible: ensayos desde un presente en crisis*, Tinta Limón, 2018, pp. 13–91.

Rivera Cusicanqui, Silvia. "Violencias encubiertas en Bolivia." *Violencias (re)encubiertas en Bolivia*, Mirada Salvaje, 2010, pp. 33–114.

Sabina, María. "Vida." *Selections*, edited by Jerome Rothenberg, University of California Press, 2003.

Saldaña-Portillo, Josefina. "Who's the Indian in Aztlan? Re-Writing Mestizaje, Indianism, and Chicanismo from the Lacandon." *The Latin American Subaltern Studies Reader*, edited by Iliana Yamileth Rodriguez, Duke University Press, 2020, pp. 402–423, 10.1515/9780822380771.

Segato, Rita. "Género y colonialidad: del patriarcado comunitario de baja intensidad al patriarcado colonial moderno de alta intensidad." *La crítica de la colonialidad en ocho ensayos*, Prometeo, 2018, pp. 69–99.
"Selection Criteria." American Library Association Tools, Publications & Resources, 19 Dec. 2017, https://www.ala.org/tools/challengesupport/selectionpolicytoolkit/criteria.
"Services, Sales & Rights." HarperCollins Publishers, https://www.harpercollins.com/pages/services-sales-rights.
"Sobre nosotrxs." Taller Leñateros, https://tallerlenateros.com/qui%C3%A9nes-somos-1.
Stein, Sharon. *Unsettling the University: Confronting the Colonial Foundations of US Higher Education*. Johns Hopkins UP, 2022.
Stradanus, Johannes. "Jan van Der Straet, Called Stradanus: Allegory of America." *The Metropolitan Museum of Art*, https://www.metmuseum.org/art/collection/search/343845.
Tallbear, Kim. "A Sharpening of the Already Present: Settler Apocalypse 2020." *YouTube*, uploaded by David J Kahane, 9 Oct. 2020, https://www.youtube.com/watch?v=eO14od9mlTA.
Tallbear, Kim. "Beyond Diversity & Inclusion to Decolonization in Science, Technology, and Policy." *YouTube*, uploaded by Institute for Integrative Conservation, 4 Feb. 2022, https://www.youtube.com/watch?v=GMxiZBRi8nk.
Tallbear, Kim. "Feminist, Queer, and Indigenous Thinking as an Antidote to Masculinist Objectivity and Binary Thinking in Biological Anthropology." *American Anthropologist*, vol. 121, no. 2, Jan. 2019, pp. 494–496.
Tallbear, Kim, and Angela Willey. "Critical Relationality: Queer, Indigenous, and Multispecies Belonging Beyond Settler Sex & Nature." *Imaginations: Journal of Cross-Cultural Media Studies*, vol. 10, no. 1, Jul. 2019, pp. 5–15.
The Daughter of the Lake. Directed by Ernesto Cabellos, Peru, 2015.
"The United Nations Permanent Forum on Indigenous Issues." United Nations, https://www.un.org/development/desa/indigenouspeoples/wp-content/uploads/sites/19/2018/04/Indigenous-Languages.pdf.
Thomas, Paul. "Reverting Hegemonic Ideology: Research Librarians and Information Professionals as 'Critical Editors' of Wikipedia." *College & Research Libraries*, vol. 82, Jun. 2021, pp. 567–583, 10.5860/crl.82.4.567.
Tróchez Tunubalá, Luis. Na misak. *YouTube*, uploaded by RTVCPlay, 20 Aug. 2019, https://www.youtube.com/watch?v=soV3s2f0IJw
Tuck, Eve, and K. Wayne Yang. "Decolonization Is Not a Metaphor." *Decolonization: Indigeneity, Education & Society*, vol. 1, no. 1, 2012, pp. 1–40.
United States, Copyright Office. *U.S. Copyright Office Fair Use Index*. https://www.copyright.gov/fair-use/.
Valdebenito, Rafael. "Feria del Libro Mapuche Huilliche abre sus puertas en Osorno." *Diario de Osorno*, 22 Jun. 2023, https://www.diariodeosorno.cl/noticia/panoramas-y-cultura/2023/06/feria-del-libro-mapuche-huilliche-abre-sus-puertas-en-osorno.
Wolf, Eric R. "Aspects of Group Relations in a Complex Society: Mexico." *American Anthropologist*, vol. 58, no. 6, 1956, pp. 1065–1078.
Wu, Shuheng. "Implementing Bibliographic Enhancement Data in Academic Library Catalogs: An Empirical Study." *Cataloging & Classification Quarterly*, vol. 61, no. 3–4, May 2023, pp. 308–345, 10.1080/01639374.2023.2224781.
Yuan, Weijing, Marlene Van Ballegooie, and Jennifer L. Robertson. "Ebooks Versus Print Books: Format Preferences in an Academic Library." *Collection Management*, vol. 43, no. 1, Jan. 2018, pp. 28–48, 10.1080/01462679.2017.1365264.

Index

Abiayala 3, 9–10, 15–6, 63–5, 78, 80, 82
Acuña, Máxima 66
Africa 5, 10, 16n2; African internationalism 11
Afro-descendants 51
Allen, Paula Gunn 76–77
Amazon (company) 30, 32, 41–3, 45
Amazon rainforest 16
Andes 16, 17n3, 21, 51, 65–8, 74, 81, 83n1
animation (film genre) 25
Aniñir, David 21–2, 35n7
Anthropocene 1, 15, 16n1, 59, 66
Apache 35n15
approval plans 30, 32–3, 36n26
Arapaho (Native American peoples) 10
area studies 48, 54–5, 58
Argentina 34, 78, 81
Arguedas, José María 21, 57
Aymara 5, 11, 22–4

Barnes & Noble (company) 30, 42
bibliographic enhancement data (BIBED) 37, 42–4, 46
bilingual: bilingual authors 22; bilingual books 22, 24, 35n11, 39, 43–4; bilingual education 12, 82; bilingual film 73; bilingual Indigenous women 69, 76
Blackness 16
Bolivia 65, 81
book fairs 32–4
book vendors 18–9, 30–1, 33, 36n23, 38–9

Camsá 22
capitalism 3–4, 54, 60, 76–7
Celebrating the Indigenous Americas (CU-Boulder) 33, 82

Cherokee 10, 19, 29
Chicanx 69, 81; Chicanx studies 52, 55–6
Chickasaw 13
Chile 22, 24–5, 31, 34, 35n7
Colchado Lucio, Óscar 34
Colonialism: anticolonial 65, 78; colonial biases/distortions 26, 67; colonial dynamics/ideologies/power 10, 13, 15, 51–3, 55, 62–3, 70; colonial foundations of US academia 49; colonial history/legacy 63–4; colonial state/system/societies 5, 8, 63, 76–7; colonialist terminology in libraries 44; European invasion/colonization of the Americas 4–6, 8; external colonialism 9, 57, 63, 65, 71–2; linguistic colonization/coloniality 15, 64; postcolonial 6, 70; settler/internal colonialism 2, 15, 17n2, 53, 55, 57, 63, 65, 71–2, 73
Coloniality: coloniality/modernity 15, 16n1, 60, 74; coloniality of the curriculum (Fúnez-Flores, Jairo) 14–5, 48, 61n3; coloniality of gender (Lugones, María) 7, 61n2, 64, 72–3, 76–7; coloniality of power (Quijano, Aníbal) 4, 8, 48, 51–2, 55, 61n2, 66–7, 77; epistemic coloniality 11
Columbus, Christopher 4–5, 7
copyright 27–8; Copyright Act 27; fair use 27–8, 36n18
Cree 120
criollo 6, 51, 54, 56–8, 65
cultural broker 38–41
curriculum 1–2, 4, 9–10, 14–15, 19, 24, 26–7, 29, 34, 40, 48–50, 53, 58, 62,

68–9, 80–2; curriculum design 2, 9; liberal arts curriculum 49; non-hegemonic curriculum 34, 49

Daughter of the Lake 15, 65–6, 69–70
De la Cadena, Marisol 1, 5, 11–2, 35n8, 56–7, 59–60
decolonization 2–3, 10–1, 18, 32, 49, 64, 70, 78; decolonial approach/critique/framework 1–2, 4, 7, 32, 48, 60; decolonization as metaphor 1, 49, 65, 71; decolonial praxis/struggle 3, 10, 58; decolonizing the curriculum 14–5, 49–50, 54, 60, 69
digital book/collection 14, 31, 37–8, 42, 45–6
discoverability of materials 14, 37, 41, 44, 46
diversity 15, 25, 40–1, 52, 58, 74; diversity, equity, and inclusion (DEI), critique of 1, 62

environment: environmental justice 63, 65; food cultivation/security/sovereignty 12, 20, 66, 68, 76, 82; green colonialism 63, 68; Indigenous activist for land and environmental rights 1, 65–6; land conservation 20, 25; medicinal plants/ancestral medicine 12, 66; sustainability/land conservation 20, 25
ethnic studies 48, 53–5, 58
ethnography: ethnographic approach 18; ethnographic film 25–6, 35n15
European/Eurocentric 2–3, 6–7, 10, 14–15, 49–51, 53, 57–60, 67
extractivism 1–2, 5

faculty 2, 12–4, 27–9, 37–41, 44, 46, 48, 50–2, 54, 60n1, 68, 82
feminism: Indigenous/Indigenizing feminism 15, 63–4; Western feminism 65, 78
film *see also* teaching films (courses/screenings); film producers/creators 3, 13, 18, 25, 35n13, 63–5, 67, 69, 74; Indigenous films/cinema 9, 18, 24, 26–9, 53, 64, 67, 71; public performance rights 27–8, 36n18
Fúnez-Flores, Jairo *see* Coloniality of the curriculum

Global North 2–3, 9, 15, 16n2, 63–5, 68, 70–1
Global South 2–3, 16n2, 49, 63–5, 70–1
Google (company) 41–2
Guamán Poma de Ayala, Felipe, *The First New Chronicle and Good Government* 7–9
Guarani 11, 59

healing 13, 15, 18, 34, 62–3, 70, 78; healing justice (McCaslin, Wanda D. and Denise C. Breton) 62–3, 68, 70, 78; Indigenous healing methods 67
Herlihy-Mera, Jeffrey 50–1, 60n1
Hispanismo 14, 50–4
Humboldt, Alexander von 5

Inca 5
Incommensurability 12, 15, 59, 68–9
Indian 4–6, 17n3, 17n4, 21, 35n8, 44, 56, 72; Indian/Indigenous 5–6, 17n3; Federal Indian Policy Act 77
indigenismo 54–8
Indigenous: alliances between Indigenous and non-Indigenous peoples 3, 9, 34; Global Indigeneity 82; Indigenous authors/scholars/writers 3–4, 7, 13, 18, 20, 22–3, 25, 30–1, 33, 39–40, 46, 63–4; Indigenous knowledge/epistemologies 3–4, 8–13, 15, 19–21, 24, 29, 33–4, 40, 46, 50, 57–60, 63, 66, 81; Indigenous languages 10–2, 14–5, 18, 21, 23, 26, 32, 39, 41–2, 44, 51, 53–4, 60, 62–4, 69, 78, 80–2; Indigenous literature 18–24, 26, 29–34, 34n2, 35n14, 36n23, 37–8, 40–1, 43, 45–6; Indigenous materials/collections 1–3, 7, 9–10, 13–5, 20, 24, 32, 38, 41, 44, 49, 52–3, 55, 58; Indigenous sexual dissidence/homosexuality 15, 73, 76–7; Indigenous women 63–5, 66–9, 76, 78
insider knowledge/perspective 24–7
intercultural/cross-cultural exchange 9, 12, 15, 18, 22, 27, 59–60
Ixcanul 53, 71–3

Justice, Daniel Heath 19, 29

Keme, Emil 3, 9, 64, 82
Kimmerer, Robin Wall; *Braiding Sweetgrass* 19–20, 35n3, 59; gift 13, 19–20, 34, 49, 56, 58

knowledge: agents of knowledge 2–3, 7, 9, 11, 49, 52, 69; geopolitics of knowledge 4, 9, 54; knowledge production and distribution 2–3, 7–9, 14, 48–50, 54, 58, 63, 67; pluriversal knowledge 10–3, 59, 78

Lakota 10, 64
land see also Mariátegui, José Carlos; dispossession of land/material dispossession 3–4, 7, 15–16, 29, 48–9, 53, 63–5, 69–72, 78, 81; land ownership/reclamation/struggle 12, 19, 63–5, 66, 68, 71, 77–8, 79n4
language reclamation/revitalization 10, 12–3, 17n3, 18, 53, 58, 64, 69
Latin America 1–2, 9, 15–16, 16n2, 17n3, 18, 20–2, 26, 30, 32–3, 46, 50, 52, 54–7, 61n3, 64, 71–4; Latin American and Latinx studies 14, 33, 50, 54–5, 58, 67, 80–1, 83n2; Latin American studies 11, 14, 54–5, 83n1
Latinoamericanismo 53–4, 56, 58
Latinx 1–2, 14–6, 48, 50–6, 58, 61n1, 73, 80; Afro-Latinx 56; Chicanx 52, 55; Critical Latinx Indigeneities studies 15, 54–6, 72; Indigenous Latinx 2, 15–6, 48, 50, 56, 58, 80; Latinx studies 54–5
Lempert, William 25–6, 35n15 see also insider knowledge/perspective
Lenca 65
library: library catalog 41–4; library collection 2, 13–4, 18–9, 48; youth collection 24
librarian 2, 13–4, 18–20, 23–4, 27–30, 32–4, 34n1, 36n18, 37–41, 44, 46, 48, 54
LibraryThing (company) 41, 43
librero (book vendor) 13, 19, 30, 32–4
literature see also Indigenous literature; literary canon 14, 37–9, 45, 51, 54, 82; literary genres 13, 23–5, 31, 34n2, 43
Lugones, Maria see coloniality of gender

Mama Irene, Healer of the Andes 66
Mapuche 21–2, 25, 34, 35n7, 76, 78
Mapudungun 11, 22, 26, 35n10, 64
Mariátegui, Jose Carlos 66
Maya 5, 11, 22–3, 45, 73; Maya Kaqchikel 53, 64; Maya K'iche' 3

Mazatec 23
Mbembe, Achilles 10–1
McCaslin, Wanda D. and Denise C. Breton see healing justice
mestizaje 14, 54–8, 74; mestizo 21–2, 24, 26, 35n8, 51, 56–7, 58, 65, 72
Mexica 5
Mexico 23, 31–4, 36n23, 38, 72, 83n2; Guatemala-Mexico border 58; Mexico-US border 56, 58, 82
Migration/migrant experiences 15–6, 22, 38, 55–6, 58, 63, 68, 72–3, 82
Millán, Moira 76, 78
Misak 25
Miskito 39
Mixtec 22
Mothers of the Land/Sembradoras de la vida 15, 41, 66–8
Musqueam 44, 47n6
Myaamia/Miami 10

Nahuatl 11, 22, 24, 32
nation-state 4, 11, 14, 48, 54, 57–8, 78
natural language processing (NLP) 42
Navajo 10
neoliberalism 1, 49, 52

Oyěwùmí, Oyèrónkẹ́, *The Invention of Women* 76–7, 79n4

Paiute 67, 69
patriarchy 63, 73, 75–7; anti-patriarchal struggle as anti-colonial 78; patriarchy of low-intensity 79n4
Peru 8, 21, 25, 31, 56–7, 65–7, 71, 81, 83n1
Potawatomi 13, 19, 59
publishing industries: editoriales/casas editoras 31–4, 36n22; fondos culturales 31; large commercial/hegemonic publishers 2, 13, 30, 40; multilingual editions 22, 24, 35n11, 37; self-publication 30; small/independent/non-mainstream publishers 19, 30, 32, 40
Puerto Rico 50
purchase: acquisition practices 20, 23, 26–30, 33–4, 36n26, 37–41, 46; purchase suggestion 34n1

QINTI group 81–2
Quechua: Quechua films 64, 67–9, 73–4, 81; Quechua Film Series

(CU-Boulder) 67, 74; Quechua language 11, 17n5, 21–4, 41, 53, 64, 67–9, 73–4, 81; Quechua language classes/instruction 12, 68–9, 74, 80–1, 83n1; Quechua Language Program (CU-Boulder) 15, 80–2, 83n2; Quechua oral literature 21; Quechua people/speakers 12, 16, 21–2, 68–9, 75–6, 79n2, 80–1, 83n1; Quechua reader 35n11, 51; writing/works in Quechua 21–4
Quijano, Anibal *see* coloniality of power
quipu 7–9

racialization/racialized people 5, 7, 21, 25, 35n6, 48–9, 55–6, 58
reader 18–20, 23–4, 30, 35, 40, 43
Retablo 15, 53, 71, 73–4
Rivera Cusicanqui, Silvia 2, 32

Sabina, María 23–4
search engine 14, 42
Segato, Rita *see* patriarchy of low-intensity
social media 32
Spain 4, 8, 50–2, 60n1, 61n3, 66
stakeholders 13, 30–4, 40
Stradanus, Johannes (*Allegory of America*) 6–7
Sumaq Kawsay (Good Living) 66, 68

Taino 7
Tallbear, Kim 16n1, 62, 79n5
teaching *see also* language reclamation/revitalization; heritage language teaching 12, 52; second-language teaching/acquisition 12, 48, 51, 74; Spanish language teaching 11, 54, 74; teaching film (courses/screening) 14, 2–8, 36n18, 53, 64, 81–2; teaching gender and indigeneity 14, 64–5; teaching Indigenous languages 10–2, 62–3, 80; teaching materials 15, 81; teaching methodologies 13
Tzotzil 23

United Nations 4
United States of America 11, 14–5, 17n2, 18, 22, 27, 30–1, 35n18, 37, 50, 52, 54–6, 65, 69, 71–3, 81–2

Vallejo, César 21, 57–8
Velasco, Alvarado 66

window: "open window" as metaphor 14, 37, 39
Winnemucca, Sarah 69–70

Yanomami (Indigenous peoples) 26–7

Zapotec 11, 22, 24, 43–4

For Product Safety Concerns and Information please contact our EU representative GPSR@taylorandfrancis.com
Taylor & Francis Verlag GmbH, Kaufingerstraße 24, 80331 München, Germany

www.ingramcontent.com/pod-product-compliance
Lightning Source LLC
Chambersburg PA
CBHW051758230426
43670CB00012B/2347